# Special Curricular Needs

# Special Curricula Needs

Edited by
**Keith Bovair**
**Barry Carpenter**
**Graham Upton**

**David Fulton Publishers**
**and**
**NASEN**
**National Association for Special Educational Needs**

David Fulton Publishers Ltd
2 Barbon Close, London WCIN 3JX

First published in Great Britain by
David Fulton Publishers 1992,
in association with the National Association for Special Educational Needs

Note: The right of the contributors to be identified as the authors of their work
has been asserted by them in accordance with the Copyright, Designs and Patents
Act 1988.

*British Library Cataloguing in Publication Data*

A catalogue record for this book is
available from the British Library

ISBN 1-85346-216-0 ✓

Typeset by Chapterhouse, Formby L37 3PX
Printed in Great Britain by BPCC Wheatons Ltd., Exeter.

# Contents

# Contributors

**Keith Bovair** is a Lecturer in Special Education and Educational Psychology at the University of Birmingham. Previously he was Headteacher of the Lady Adrian School for children with moderate learning difficulties in Cambridge.

**Erica Brown** is National Co-ordinator for R.E. and special educational needs. She has taught in ordinary and special schools, has been involved in the in-service training of teachers and has written widely about R.E. and special educational needs.

**Richard Byers** is currently seconded from his teaching post at Riverwalk School in Bury St. Edmunds in order to support curriculum development in Suffolk County Council's schools for pupils with learning difficulties. During 1990 and 1991 he was a member of the National Development Team based at Cambridge Institute of Education.

**Barry Carpenter** is Inspector for Schools for Solihull Education Authority with particular responsibility for special educational needs. Until recently he was Headteacher of Blythe School in Warwickshire.

**John Clarke** is Senior Adviser (Monitoring and Evaluation) in Suffolk LEA where he was previously Humanities Adviser. He has taken a strong interest in strategies to meet individual needs in the History and Geography curriculum and was joint author of 'Humanities for All'.

**Caroline Hammond** is Learning Support Co-ordinator in Manor Comprehensive School, Nottingham. She has worked extensively in special and ordinary schools but has a particular interest in supporting young people in the mainstream.

**Linda Howe** is Headteacher of a primary school in Suffolk. Before taking this post she was Advisory Teacher for Primary Science in Suffolk in which capacity she worked in special and ordinary schools.

**Sean McCavera** is a teacher at the Vale School for pupils with physical disabilities in Haringey, North London. he previously taught in inner city viii

comprehensive schools and at a school for children with moderate learning difficulties.

**Ruth Nichols** was formerly Adviser for Special Education for Berkshire and is now Senior Inspector, Special Educational Needs.

**Geoffrey Read** is Deputy Headteacher in Derrymount School, a school for children with learning difficulties in Nottingham. He has a particular interest in curriculum access for all children which he has pursued as an area of research and which has lead to a heavy involvement in staff development.

**Phillip Rodbard** is Deputy Manager of Further Education at St. Piers Lingfield, a residential special school catering for epilepsy and other neurological disorders. He was formerly a research fellow and associate lecturer in education at Brunel University.

**David Sugden** is a Reader in the School of Education at the University of Leeds. His special interests lie in the fields of motor development and impairment and the cognitive strategies of children with learning difficulties. He has extensive teaching experience in Britain and the USA.

**Rod Taylor** is Art Adviser for Wigan Local Education Authority and Director of Drumcroon Education Art Centre. From 1981 to 1984 he was Director of the national Critical Studies in Art Education Project. He has written widely on a range of issues in Art Education.

**Gwen Thomas** teaches French language and literature in the Department of French Studies at the University of Reading. She was formerly in the Modern Languages Department of Bulmershe College of Higher Education.

**Graham Upton** is Professor of Education and Head of the School of Education at the University of Birmingham. He has undertaken research and published extensively and has a special interest in the education of children with emotional and behavioural difficulties.

**Barrie Wade** is a Senior Lecturer in the School of Education at the University of Birmingham. He has published extensively in the fields of language in education and special educational needs as well as writing poetry, fiction and non-fiction for children.

**Klaus Wedell** is Professor in the Education of Children with Special Needs at the Institute of Education, University of London. He has written and carried out research on a wide range of special needs topics and in the field of professional educational psychology.

**Alec Williams** taught in primary and residential special schools before serving as headmaster of an all-age school for pupils with moderate learning difficulties and subsequently as tutor to one-year special needs courses at the University of Hull and at Bishop Grosseteste College, Lincoln.

**Michael Wilson** is Deputy Head of Carr Mill 11–18 High School, Kirkham, Lancashire. He has contributed to in-service training courses for teachers and has written a number of articles on history teaching and a book on the teaching of history to children with learning difficulties.

# *Acknowledgements*

During the past three years the *British Journal of Special Education* has published a large number of articles which have addressed issues concerning the education of pupils with special educational needs raised by the introduction of the National Curriculum. The contents of the book are a selection of those articles which have focused on the core and foundation subjects and cross curricula themes. Although articles have been updated to ensure their relevance to the most recent thinking about the National Curriculum the editors are indebted to Margaret Peter, the editor of the *British Journal of Special Education*, for her work in the identification of authors and structuring of the original contributions. Without her initiative this book would not exist.

# INTRODUCTION

# The Whole Curriculum: Meeting the Needs of the Whole Child

*Barry Carpenter*

## Exploring the whole curriculum

The Warnock Report emphasised that the goals of education were the same for all children. This is absolutely true, providing that these goals are then balanced, and brought into harmony with the individual needs of the child. Meeting individual needs is about careful planning and room organisation coupled with a positive, caring ethos where children are able to feel confident and safe.

Much is written in current curriculum literature about entitlement. Children with special educational needs are 'entitled' to have their individual needs met, but a blanket delivery of a rigid, subject-bound curriculum may not be the most effective means of achieving this.

Entitlement is an underlying principle for many of the recent initiatives in education (i.e. TVEI, Records of Achievement), and it is particularly pertinent in relation to the National Curriculum. If we accept this entitlement for children with special educational needs then the onus rests with us, as special educators, to define the degrees of access needed to make our children active participants within their curriculum. This will demand of us reflection upon how we compose the whole curriculum for the child matched to their learning needs; a re-examination of our teaching styles; modification of the traditional curriculum terminology that has been distinctively associated with special education.

Access for children with special educational needs to the National Curriculum will require their teachers to devise imaginative and innovative learning routes. These learning routes will need to embrace all the key elements upon which the National Curriculum has been built – breadth, balance, relevance and differentiation. But that is right and proper. A broadly-based curriculum is essential; special educational needs are not in themselves an excuse for a narrowness of curriculum experience. 'Balance' is an issue that is a timely reminder that we should not allow the nature of a child's special needs to blinker our vision, and deprive the child of a richness of learning experiences.

Balance should be achieved in relation to the needs of the individual. Circular 22/89 (DES) empowers schools to devise a curriculum programme for the child that responds to needs, and the Statement of Special Educational Needs is the vehicle for doing this. Traditionally Special Educators have thought of themselves as devising well-documented curricula, equally as detailed as any National Curriculum document produced to date. (Although recent research from Bennett (1991) would dispute this.) Nevertheless, where it is necessary, in order to meet the child's highly specific learning needs, to use sources other than the National Curriculum we have sufficient skills as special educators to generate the appropriate curriculum materials and programmes. Through this process, and the flexibility given by the legal requirements of the 1981 Education Act, we can achieve balance for each individual child with special educational needs.

Relevance is not a new notion in Special Education. How long have we stressed the need for age-appropriate curricula and the fact that it does nothing to enhance the personal dignity of 15 year old students with special needs if they are seen carrying out a Mathematics activity from Key Stage 2 with apparatus intended for an 8 year old? We must strive to ensure that our children with special needs are indeed given relevant learning experiences, and that because many of them will operate in the early levels of National Curriculum, they are not taught through methods and approaches more suited to infant/junior age pupils.

## A differentiated response

Differentiation is synonymous with good teaching (Moore, 1992). The whole thrust of the learning situations that we present to our pupils should enable them, regardless of their different backgrounds and abilities, to demonstrate what they know, understand and are able to do. H.M.I. (1986) stressed that teachers should ensure that pupils are given tasks which are commensurate with their level of attainment, ensuring that pupils achieve success and feel that learning experiences have been worthwhile.

The strength of special educators has been their ability to respond to the needs of the individual. With the emphasis in the National Curriculum on a differentiated curriculum, all teachers need to be aware of the individual learning needs of children in their classes. For too long we have looked for the source of learning difficulties 'within' the child. Now, through the National Curriculum we are having to thoroughly re-appraise the whole curriculum and examine our teaching styles. As Smith (1982) says:

> If children find learning difficult, it could well be that there is something wrong with the way we are asking them to learn, rather than something the matter with their innate capacity for learning.

King (1990) argues that through our audit of the curriculum we will come to realise the potential of differentiation as the key to a whole range of curriculum experiences for all children: 'differentiation is about meeting the needs of all learners and requires a concern with the pupil, the task and the learning context'. No longer must we view differentiation as the territory of those who teach the less able (Spillman, 1991). All learners are different and all teaching needs to be differentiated. It is through the strength of differentiation that children with special educational needs will be given access to the curriculum, and that continuity and progression will be ensured (Ashdown, Carpenter and Bovair, 1991).

A major concern of teachers has been that the National Curriculum will become a curriculum straight-jacket. The reality of this concern has caused a biased focus on only the core and foundation subjects which in turn, has given rise to 'Mad Academic Disease' (Wragg, 1990). This disease is fatal to the education of children with special educational needs. The antidote is the 'Whole Curriculum': a curriculum diet that feeds and sustains the whole child, rather than causing global malnourishment through experiences which fail to give sustenance. For, as the then Secretary of State, John MacGregor, re-affirmed (July 1990):

> the National Curriculum is not inflexible nor is it all-embracing. It is a sure and rigorous foundation on which all teachers can build using their professional skills and judgement and to which other important elements . . . must be added.

A key issue, often overlooked in the current debate about the National Curriculum is that of coherence. We must ensure our children are not given a fragmented curricular experience, through our endeavours to apply the National Curriculum to them. Their learning needs, in all areas of development, must be our starting point. In this sense cross-curricula approaches may be helpful for adding a framework to the total curriculum package devised for each child (NCC, 1989). As certain curriculum areas take on a new indentity (i.e. Technology) or receive a raised profile (i.e. Science) in the curriculum then we must try to avoid compartmentalizing the child and his/her curriculum into neat pockets of learning. If the core and foundation subjects are to be the building blocks in the curriculum then the cross-curricular elements are the cement which hold it all together. To this end, coherence must be our watchword.

4

**Curriculum compatibility**

A driving force in the traditional design of the Special Educational Needs Curriculum has been the goal of personal autonomy for each child. To make the child as independent as possible was seen as a primary target, and significant attention has been given to the design and composition of the curriculum for the later years, culminating in such strategies as the 'Leavers' Programme', Life Skills courses, and PSE programmes.

This goal of autonomy must be retained! How do we go about this in the context of a National Curriculum which seems to be heavily skewed towards academic capabilities? We must now seek to chart a route in the 'new' curriculum that will enable the child with learning difficulties to achieve maximum personal autonomy. The independence of the child must be an outcome of the educational process. It must remain high on the agenda of all involved in the education of children with special educational needs, but as usual teachers will be the advocates, in particular, for this cause. Indeed, many young people with learning difficulties are realistic about their own aspirations for independence post-school in the areas of work, leisure and housing. Circular 22/89 now provides those who are Statemented with a strategy, through the Annual Review procedure, where they can vocalise and negotiate the ambitions which will lead them to their autonomy.

The Education Reform Act 1988, placed a statutory responsibility upon schools to provide a broad and balanced curriculum which prepares pupils for the opportunities, responsibilities and experiences of adult life. Here we find, implicit in the the 1988 Act, the prime motivating goal of Special Educational Needs. HMI (1990) similarly emphasises that we must ensure that the curriculum serves the child in 'promoting personal development and preparing the pupil for adult life'.

*Curriculum Guidance Three: The Whole Curriculum* (NCC, 1990a), illuminates the context against which the National Curriculum must be set through its discussion of cross-curricular skills, dimensions and themes. Many of the fears of the special educator that the child with learning difficulties may be forced to follow an arid academic curriculum, are put to rest. The need for all elements of the curriculum to contribute to the personal and social education (PSE) of all pupils is stressed in this document. PSE has a major role to play in the education of all children, but for the child with special needs it is vital that it is dealt with thoroughly and in considerable depth. The cross-curricular elements afford enrichment and diversity to the overall curriculum experience.

The skills identified by the National Curriculum Council as having cross-curricular application are also highly pertinent to the educational objectives embedded in the individual learning programme of the child with special needs. These skills can be fostered across the whole curriculum and comprise communication, numeracy, problem-solving, personal, information technology, and modern foreign language. The development of these skills in young people is directly aligned to preparation for adulthood: 'What is beyond dispute is that in the next century these skills, together with flexibility and adaptability, will be at a premium'. (NCC, 1990a).

The 'themes' outlined by the National Curriculum Council are particularly noteworthy for the special educator. It is to be regretted that these were not issued prior to the publication of the core subjects, for it is here that curriculum compatibility can be achieved. The cross-curricular skills, dimensions and themes should form the bedrock upon which we set the core and foundation subjects of the National Curriculum. Mirrored in the details explaining careers education and guidance, economic and industrial understanding etc., we can find may of the curriculum activities we have considered crucial to the education of the child with learning difficulties. What is more, these activities are given status, and are accepted in their own right as valid and valuable. We are no longer left thinking that subversive activity will be necessary to facilitate the achievement of these targets for our children with special needs.

It will be possible to openly state where the themes are contributing to the total educational package for the child. Indeed, the curriculum weighting towards these themes may be greater for the child with special needs. Whilst it is appreciated that as cross-curricular themes they are intended to be delivered across the core and foundation subjects, it may be necessary to maintain consistent relevance to the child's individual needs, to elaborate, consolidate and extend some of the key messages in these themes through discrete sessions.

Readers can, by referring to *Curriculum Guidance 3*, examine the details and implications of this document for children with special needs. However, a few phrases which offer 'light in our darkness', and words of reassurance, may be helpful.

In the latter years of school a key experience has been, wherever possible, work experience, and this is of tremendous value to the less able child. The economic and industrial understanding theme says that 'pupils should have direct experience of industry and the world of work' (NCC, 1990b).

Activities proposed for Key Stages one and two such as shopping, or investigating a local facility, would, if planned sensitively and in an age-appropriate manner, be pertinent for pupils in Key Stage four also.

Recently, a group of pupils with special educational needs planned a Christmas party for a group of senior citizens. This involved them not only in the costing and purchasing of food within a limited budget, but also in a 'needs' identification of the eating habits of old people. Why would coke and crisps not be the choice of old people? What should the entertainment be? The students' first choice was a Disco, but again further exploration showed that the choice of some of the senior citizens was for a bingo-caller, or an old-time music hall singer. All salutary learning experiences for young people!

Self-esteem is of paramount importance to the child with special needs; often their educational failure at some point in their school career may have jeopardised this. It is heartening therefore, to read that careers education and guidance 'aims first of all to help pupils to develop self-awareness'. This is fundamental to the personal growth and development of all children, and may be achieved through a variety of strategies according to the nature of the child's learning difficulties. For the student with emotional and behavioural difficulties it may be through counselling approaches; for the child with profound and multiple learning difficulties it may be through the sensory curriculum.

The range of interesting learning opportunities detailed in *Curriculum Guidance 6* (NCC, 1990d) challenges our traditional interpretation of Careers Education and Guidance. For example, in Key Stage one pupils can plan a visit to a workplace (local factory, farm, fire station, café, bus depot), decide information needed, devise questions to ask and items to be collected (timetables, pictures, leaflets). At Key Stage three pupils could carry out a self-assessment exercise (strengths and weaknesses, likes and dislikes, independence of mind, self-discipline, self-confidence).

Health education is seen as the umbrella for a range of issues, all of which are highly relevant to the child with special needs: sex education, family life education, safety, nutrition, personal hygiene etc. Apart from inculcating in the child the need for a healthy mind and body, this theme sets about developing 'an appreciation and understanding of responsibilities to the community'.

The learning opportunities presented in the Health Education document (NCC, 1990c) offer essential material for all pupils, but in reading it one is struck by the strong parallels which arise with the key experiences that have traditionally been blended into courses for pupils with special needs. Personal hygiene (Key Stage 1) indicates that pupils should understand the need for and be able to practice simple personal routines e.g. washing hands, cleaning teeth, using a handkerchief. (All of these will be particularly recognisable to the teacher in special education!). At Key Stage 4 crucial skills such as safety appear with the expectation that if pupils are to live independently in their own homes eventually they should be able to demonstrate safe practices in various environments (e.g. home, work, etc.).

This leads well into the notion of responsible citizenship developed by the theme, 'Education for Citizenship'. The outline of this theme, covering citizens' rights, leisure education, work and employment, family and parenting etc., is in itself a major component of some of the courses offered to students with special needs in their later years of school. It is encouraging to see these key elements so clearly endorsed, and set against the scenario of a broader curriculum context than may traditionally have been envisaged for the delivery of these crucial topics.

Some of activities nominated in the Education for Citizenship document

(NCC, 1990f) facilitate learning at an individual level or in a small or whole group. For example, in Key Stage 3 students could be given personal responsibilities such as acting as a class representative or organising extra-curricular events. A small group may chose to organise a fundraising event for a local charity or international cause. At a whole school level activities may take the form of hosting a group of visitors or assuming collective responsibility for an aspect of school or community life, e.g. keeping the school grounds free of litter, publishing a community newsletter etc.

Environmental issues are the responsibility of every citizen, and those with learning difficulties should be no exception to this. Environmental education 'is concerned with promoting positive and responsible attitudes towards the environment'. (NCC, 1990e). As such it is pertinent to develop positive and mindful attitudes in all children from an early age.

In Key Stage 1 a Nature Trail activity is suggested. This would be pitched according to the chronological age of the group to be involved. Younger pupils may be encouraged to use their senses in the discovery of the natural world, e.g. touching the trees and feeling the texture of the various types of bark. Older pupils may name plants or talk about conservation issues such as keeping to paths on public walks, exploring their own developing sense of public responsibility.

## Conclusion

What follows in this book is a review of the core and foundation subjects of the National Curriculum. As Cross Curricular issues are so crucial to the effective delivery of the National Curriculum a section on this has been included. Likewise, Assessment features large on every teacher's agenda currently, and this issue is debated in the final section of the book.

The list of chapters under their respective subject headings may look as if we are promoting a subject-based curriculum for pupils with special educational needs. Although the book examines separate subject strands, we are advocating a curriculum package which is responsive to meeting individual needs. Never has it been more critical that we adopt a holistic view of the curriculum. We must identify the contexts that our pupils will find themselves in (home, community, eventually work), and ensure that the learning opportunities presented to them genuinely equip them with the requisite skills, knowledge and attitudes to lead fulfilling and rewarding lives. A rigid, subject-bound academic curriculum cannot hope to achieve this. And yet if our pupils are not presented with wider opportunities than the National Curriculum alone offers, their educational experience will be impoverished.

As such a Whole Curriculum approach, encompassing the key principles of breadth, balance, relevance and differentiation, has to be key to meeting the needs of pupils with special educational needs. It is a pity that more of

8

the final subject working party reports, or indeed the subsequent statutory orders, did not advocate, as the final report on Physical Education (DES, 1991) did, that pupils with special educational needs are not only entitled to access to the subject, but that this should be delivered with integrity. It would be wrong to present our pupils with learning experiences that are demeaning because of the constraints of a National Curriculum. The personal dignity of the pupil with special needs must be preserved, and promoted at all times.

The National Curriculum poses a major challenge to all teachers, particularly those who serve the learning needs of children with special educational needs. However, in the knowledge that these highly specific needs of our children can be set in the context of the whole curriculum, the challenge seems less imposing, and the curriculum route more viable.

## References

Ashdown, R., Carpenter, B., Bovair, K. (1991), *The Curriculum Challenge*. London: Falmer Press

Bennett, N. (1991), 'The Quality of Classroom Learning Experiences for Children with Special Educational Needs' in Ainscow, M. (Ed.). *Effective Schools for All*. London: Fulton

DES, (1989), *Circular 22/89. Assessments and Statements of Special Educational Needs*. London: H.M.S.O.

DES, (1991), *Physical Education for ages 5 to 16*. London: H.M.S.O.

HMI, (1986), *The Curriculum: 5-16*. London: H.M.S.O.

HMI, (1990), *Education Observed: Special Needs Issues*. London: H.M.S.O.

King, V. (1990), 'Differentiation is the Key', *Language and Learning*, 3, 22–44.

MacGregor, J. (1990), *Speeches on Education: National Curriculum and Assessment*. Middlesex: H.M.S.O./D.E.S.

Moore, J. (1992), 'Planning for Differentiation', *Brit. J. Sp. Ed.* **19**, (1).

NCC, (1990a), *Curriculum Guidance 3: The Whole Curriculum*. York: N.C.C.

NCC, (1990b), *Curriculum Guidance 4: Education for Economic and Industrial Understanding*. York: N.C.C.

NCC, (1990c), *Curriculum Guidance 5: Health Education*. York: N.C.C.

NCC, (1990d), *Curriculum Guidance 6: Careers Education and Guidance*. York: N.C.C.

NCC, (1990e), *Curriculum Guidance 7: Environmental Education*. York: N.C.C.

NCC, (1990f), *Curriculum Guidance 8: Education for Citizenship*. York: N.C.C.

Smith, F. (1982), *Understanding Reading* (Third Edition), New York: Holt, Rinehart and Winston.

Spillman, J. (1991), 'Decoding Differentiation', *Special Children*, **44**, 7–10.

Wragg, T. (1990), 'Time for a Fling with the Cabinet', *Times Educational Supplement*, (20.7.90).

# SECTION 1 –
# THE CORE AND FOUNDATION
# SUBJECTS

# CHAPTER 1

# Science

*Linda Howe*

## Introduction

The National Curriculum for Science underlines the statutory entitlement of all pupils to a science curriculum. The establishment of science as a core subject creates the challenge of planning a curriculum where all children can participate in appropriate scientific activities. Providing access for children with special educational needs involves careful planning, adapting approaches and activities and developing schemes of work which allow for a range of responses. This chapter explores the issues raised when providing coordinated science programmes which cater for a range of abilities and needs with a particular focus on the provision which can be made in primary and special schools.

The contribution which scientific activities can make to the curriculum entitlement of children with special educational needs includes:

(1)  practical, relevant, first hand experiences;
(2)  enjoyable and challenging experiences where success does not depend on mastering a theorem or a body of knowledge;
(3)  a range of contexts which allow safe and careful exploration of the home and local environment;
(4)  opportunities for a range of responses providing appropriate experiences for varying levels of ability with easily achieved targets;
(5)  achievements which are not dependent on previously acquired number and/or language skills.

Although many pupils will experience difficulties in fully understanding concepts or developing the skills involved in some scientific tasks it is important to acknowledge that only a very small percentage of the total population acquire the level of scientific interest, knowledge and skills which is required to become a research scientist. However, for many people scientific activities can provide a vehicle for developing understanding and encouraging a 'controlled curiosity', about the world around them.

## Examining the National Curriculum for Science

The National Curriculum for Science (Revised Orders DES and Welsh Office, 1991) outlines the areas required to provide a broad and balanced science curriculum. Figure 1 shows the composition of the National Curriculum for Science. Although there is an apparent imbalance between the number of Programmes of Study and Attainment Targets for the two main components for Science (i.e. Skills and Concepts) these are equally weighted at Key Stages 1 and 2.

In establishing a science curriculum which caters for a range of needs the Programmes of Study can provide a broad framework for planning activities. The Attainment Targets draw out elements from the Programme of Study and use a series of Statements of Attainment to reflect pupil outcomes. Although there is a direct correlation between the Statements of

**Figure 1**  The National Curriculum for Science

| 4 Key Stages related to age: | Key Stage 1 : ages 5–7. Key Stage 2 : ages 7–11. Key Stage 3 : ages 11–14. Key Stage 4 : ages 14–16. |
|---|---|

| Programmes of Study P.O.S. (Broad areas of Experience). | Attainment Targets A.Ts. (Context for Activities). | Statements of Attainment S.O.As. (Pupil outcomes for Activities). |
|---|---|---|

2 main parts

| Exploration of Science (Skills) 1 P.O.S./A.T.: Sc. 1 Scientific Investigation | Knowledge and Understanding (Concepts) 3 P.O.S./A.Ts.: Sc.2: Life and Living Processes, (Living Things). Sc.3: Materials and their Properties, (Materials). Sc.4: Physical Processes, (Forces and Energy). |
|---|---|

Attainment and the Programmes of Study the statements do not reflect full coverage of all the elements. When planning schemes of work it is the use of the Programmes of Study which ensures that a full coverage of a broad, balanced science is achieved.

Devising differentiated schemes of work requires three main planning stages:

**Stage 1:** Broad yearly or two-yearly topic plans to reflect a balance between the broad areas of knowledge and understanding of science (i.e. Living Things, Materials and Forces and Energy).

**Stage 2:** Using the Programmes of Study to outline the areas of experience which children will meet when working on topics in the broad plan.

**Stage 3:** Detailed descriptions of experiences showing the activities which pupils will be engaged in and referenced to the Statements of Attainment where assessment opportunities will be created.

These stages can be incorporated into a cyclical planning process illustrated in Figure 2.

Using the stages outlined in Figure 2 helps to ensure balance is achieved between the areas of science in the knowledge and understanding component (more guidance on using these is given later in this section). Equally important is the planning for Science Attainment Target 1 which represents the skills which children will be using. These are fundamental in detail before the planning stages are fully examined.

**Figure 2** A Cyclical Planning Process

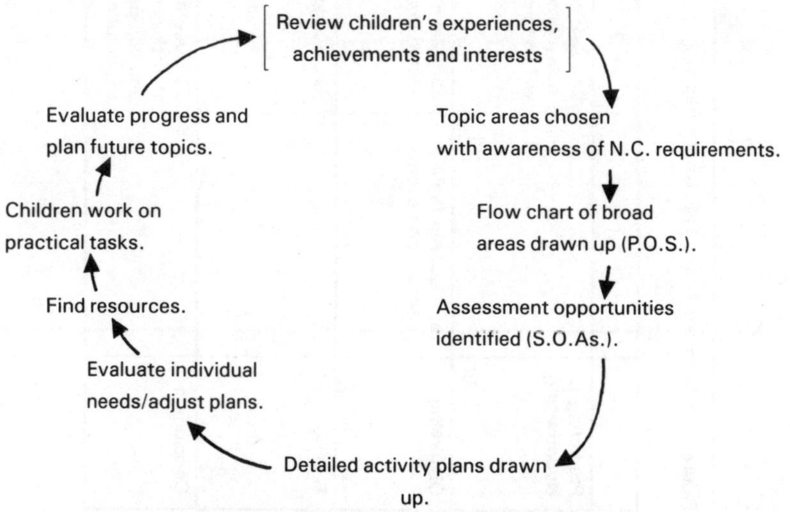

14

**Figure 3** Attainment Target 1: Scientific Skills

| | Level 1 | Level 2 | Level 3 | Level 4 | Level 5 |
|---|---|---|---|---|---|
| Predicting & Hypothesing | | 2a. Ask questions: 'how, why and what will happen if'. | 3a. Suggest testable questions, ideas and predictions. | 4a. Ask investigable questions, suggest ideas and make predictions using some knowledge. | 5a. Formulate hypothesis based on scientific knowledge, understanding and theory. |
| Observing | 1a. Observe familiar materials and events. | 2b. Make series of related observations. | 3b. Closely observe and quantify by appropriate measurement. | 4c. Identify patterns in observations. | 5b. Identify range of variables. |
| Testing | | 2a. Suggest ideas. | 3c. Recognise fair test. | 4b. Carry out fair test select and use appropriate instruments, (measuring). | 5b. Choose range of variables to produce meaningful results. |
| Concluding | | 2c. Use observation to make conclusions and compare with expectations. | 3d. Sort observations and make simple how and why explanations. | 4c. Draw conclusions looking for patterns linking predictions to results. | 5c. Evaluate conclusions considering possible interpretations. |

**Scientific skills**

Using the National Curriculum framework to plan activities across a range of abilities involves breaking down the requirements into broad steps and then breaking these down further to represent manageable activities.

Science Attainment Target 1 in Key Stages 1 and 2 can be divided into four main skill areas, namely:

(1)  Predicting and hypothesizing;
(2)  Observing;
(3)  Testing;
(4)  Drawing conclusions.

How skill areas relate to the Attainment Targets is shown in Figure 3.

These skills may appear inappropriate for some children and it is necessary to look at each area in turn to establish their relevance. In examining each skill area it becomes apparent how a range of outcomes can be seen and how the teacher can accommodate children's individual needs in schemes of work.

*Predicting and hypothesizing*

Children taking part in basic scientific activities can be encouraged to make simple predictions:

> Which car do they think will roll furthest?
> Do they think it will float?
> Which seeds will grow first?

As their responses become more confident children can be asked to group their ideas:

> Will big cars roll further than small ones?
> Will heavy or light things float best?
> Will big seeds grow into big plants?

Gradually the children can be encouraged to give reasons for their choices:

> The pink cloth will dry first because it is thin and shiny.
> My car will go best on the smooth floor because the carpet stops it going quickly.
> A round sail would be best because the wind pushes it harder.

These statements develop ideas which can be the starting point for further investigations:

> All the powders will dissolve but the other materials won't because the powders will mix into the water.
>
> Hot water and soap is best for washing dirty hands.

When children are working on explorations and investigations the expected level of predictions or hypotheses must be related to the individual child's current stage of development. This is clearly seen in a mixed ability class of six-year olds who have been asked to find the best materials to keep the Three Bears' porridge warm. A collection of materials is laid out and the children invited to choose which might be good for wrapping up the bowls. The range of responses given to questions about which they should choose and why, is illustrated in the following examples:

> I want the pink one (no reasons offered);
>
> This one is warm like my furry coat;
>
> I think the furry one would be good because it feels warm;
>
> The blanket piece is thick so the heat can't get out. I think thick pieces will be best.

Clearly some of these children will need repeated opportunities to develop ideas and build on their previous experiences whereas some are ready to extend their skills and formulate testable hypotheses:

*Observing*

Children should be encouraged to use all their senses to explore familiar objects – looking, feeling, smelling, tasting and listening. Some children find it hard to use senses in isolation (e.g. when asked what an object feels like they will describe its colour). Techniques to aid the use of the senses include:

- Sound games where sounds are made behind a screen for others to identify;
- Feeling games where children put their hands behind their backs and have an object placed in them;
- Tasting activities where foods are disguised (e.g. lemon jelly with red food colouring added).

Many children experience difficulty in identifying smells and tastes and the activity can all too easily become a memory test. When encouraging children to use their senses this can be avoided by asking them to identify pairs, e.g.:

- Cups of red drinks can be used and children asked to find two drinks which taste the same.
- Wrapped presents can be used for the identification of pairs which feel the same.
- Covered pots can be used to find pairs which smell the same.

Some children will find a wide choice bewildering and choice may need to be limited to two or three pairs. It is also important to recognise that similarities are much harder to perceive than differences. A child who is presented with a grapefruit and an orange is more likely to identify differences such as colour and size than similarities in shape or skin type. If, however, the grapefruit is placed out of sight in a bag and the child encouraged to feel it they may well say that it is an orange, recognizing that they both feel the same.

As children acquire observational skills they can be encouraged to participate in simple sorting activities starting with placing items in sets. Some children will need to begin with very basic divisions, such as 'like' and 'don't like' for tasting and smelling activities, colours for collections of materials and 'noisy' and 'quiet' for sounds. As these skills develop children can be asked to find different ways to sort a collection – e.g. a collection of gloves can be sorted by colours, plain and patterned, wool, cotton, rubber and leather, with and without separate fingers, and, possibly, stretchy and non-stretchy.

While children are involved in the sorting of items, basic ideas of measurement can be introduced. Collections can be sorted by size and simple measuring activities introduced. In this way children looking at a collection can find out which objects roll the furthest, which boxes hold most newspaper, and which sounds can be heard from furthest away. Children can start to quantify their measurements in different ways – e.g. how many foot lengths did the object roll, how many sheets of newspaper does each box hold and from how many strides away could the sound be heard?

*Testing*

Group and class tests are a useful way of involving all children in finding out and allowing each child to take the activity as far as they are able. Simple activities should concentrate on one factor:

– Which soap makes the most bubbles?
– Whose car rolls furthest?
– Which materials dry quickest?

Most children have an inherent sense of 'fairness' and this soon becomes an important element in testing activities. Sometimes teachers use extreme examples to highlight the need for 'fair testing'. An amusing incident occurred with a class of five year olds using a paved area to find which toy car went the furthest when pushed. Each child lined up with a car and on a command pushed it across the paved area. Inevitably, some cars received such a hefty push that they went right off the area, one without its wheels touching the ground, whilst others were gently pushed a few centimetres. The teacher chose the car which had gone the furthest gave it to a child whose car had only travelled a short distance. The child was asked to try again with this car and the teacher drew the children's attention to the fact that the car had only travelled a short distance this time whereas last time it had gone off the area. She asked what they thought had changed and after a thoughtful few seconds a voice volunteered, 'The sun has come out'.

Meeting different needs in activities like testing must involve a variety of working methods. Group work is particularly valuable in allowing different levels of activity around a central theme. For example, a class of children who were working on a shopping theme had visited a freezer centre. In their group they considered the problems of transporting frozen foods home without them melting and in the course of this suggested a number of ideas for tests and investigations:

- One group was concerned to find out where ice cubes melt quickest and slowest;
- One group explored the types of materials which keep wrapped ice cubes frozen for the longest time;
- Another group investigated the relationship between the number of layers used in wrapping and melting times.

In this way different groups tackled the activity in ways that were appropriate to their current level.

A basic activity can be used to provide suitable work for all of a class or group where the more able children are encouraged to extend their skills by focussing on one particular part. This can be illustrated in a situation where a class is finding out if hot or cold water is best for washing stained cloth. For many children the task of comparing the two temperatures will be sufficiently challenging. More able children, on the other hand, can find out at which temperature it is easiest to wash out different kinds of stains, extending their measuring skills by using thermometers and their investigating skills by planning their activity and limiting variables (e.g. will they use the same kind of cloth, type of stains and washing method for each test?)

*Drawing conclusions*

When children, particularly young children, are working scientifically the activity is often left open-ended without the opportunity to pull ideas together. If ideas are to be developed and extended the process of reviewing activities and sorting data which has been collected needs to become established.

A starting point for such discussion often comes from the record made during the activity. Class or group charts can be used as an introduction to recording skills and methods. These can be prepared in a way that demands few, if any, writing or drawing skills. Items or samples can be stuck on, magazine pictures or photographs used to supplement children's art work or simple techniques such as marks and name cards placed in appropriate boxes. Children who have rolled objects can stick them on a chart in order of how far they rolled. Sets of warm and cold weather clothing can be made with catalogue and children's pictures. Children can tick or place their name card next to the tastes they liked. As recording skills develop children can select and use methods suited to the activity such as using lengths of string stuck on a chart to compare how far things move; lists of substances with columns to show if the children think they will dissolve and what actually happened; and descriptive writing to specify weather observations.

These records become an integral part of the activity. The full potential is only seen, however, when these records are discussed and used to reinforce ideas. The example below shows how conclusions can be drawn at the mid-point of an activity in order to help the children to move on to the next stage.

Children have collections of containers of different shapes and sizes and a water tray. The teacher puts a small square container in the tray and asks the children how they could find out how much it will hold before it sinks. After a discussion of ideas the children decide to see how many marbles it will hold. They estimate how many and then find out. A record is made showing a drawing of the container, the estimate and the actual figure. The teacher then provides a larger square container and asks the children to repeat the activity. They are surprised at how many it will hold. The children repeat the exercise with two further square containers of different sizes. They examine their record and after a long discussion draw the conclusion that the bigger and flatter the container the more it will hold before sinking. The children test out this idea using the different shapes of containers from their collection. They complete their task and use their results when designing rafts to hold a given weight.

## Knowledge and understanding

The Programmes of Study for Science Attainment Targets 2, 3 and 4 provide a context for children to develop and use scientific skills. This section examines how structured planning ensures that children have opportunities to experience concepts in a variety of contexts.

## Stage 1: topic planning.

Careful topic planning ensures that children receive a broad, balanced range of experiences. When planning topics which meet the needs of pupils with Special Educational Needs teachers need to address three main issues:

(1)  Are the topics which I provide broad enough to cater for a range of abilities?

**Figure 4** Stage 1 A Topic Planning Device

| Broad Areas of Study | Topics which relate to these Areas | | | |
|---|---|---|---|---|
| A. Living Things (Sc.2) | Ourselves<br>Birds<br>Harvest<br>Families | Farms<br>Seasons<br>Seeds<br>Weather | Trees<br>Growth<br>Pets<br>Our School | Animals<br>Flowers<br>Litter |
| B. Materials (Sc.3) | Packaging<br>Holes<br>Changes<br>Under the Ground | Clothes<br>Food<br>Cooking | Houses<br>Hard and Soft<br>Wet and Dry<br>Things We Use | Shopping |
| C. Forces and Energy (Sc.4) | Toys<br>Fairs<br>Wheels<br>Journeys | Water<br>Ships<br>Bridges<br>Power | Moving Things<br>Up and Down<br>Making It Work<br>Sounds Around Us | |
| General Topics which can relate to any areas | Stories<br>Special Days<br>Where I Live | Colours | My World<br>Nursery Rhymes<br>Things I Like | |

(2) Are there opportunities for children to revisit areas and reinforce activities?

(3) Do I provide linked activities which allow children to develop ideas and explore materials and events?

At this stage the three main areas of knowledge and understanding are used to provide a basis for topics covered. A check list of topics matched to each of these area (see Figure 4) provides a range of contexts and a quick reference for ensuring this balance is achieved. The list is infinite and teachers can constantly update it with new titles. A topic plan is drawn up (see

**Figure 5** A 2 Year Topic Plan for Key Stage 1

| | Autumn Term | | Spring Term | | Summer Term | |
|---|---|---|---|---|---|---|
| Year 1 | Moving Things (C) | Christmas (All) | New Life (A) | Eggs (A/B) | Under the Ground (B) | Having a Picnic (All) |
| Year 2 | Toys (C) | Christmas (All) | Clothes (B) | Pets (A) | Weather (B) | Sounds Around Us (C) |
| Other Areas | Sand/water play<br>Songs and music<br>Visits<br>Weather records | | Cooking<br>Gardening<br>Art/craft | P.E., (how we move)<br>Classroom pets/plants<br>Home Corner | | |

Figure 5) using the check list, with teachers working co-operatively to ensure that the continuity of experience is transferred from one class to the next. Other areas which allow children to develop ideas and events, including those which have not previously been seen as part of the scientific curriculum, are identified and feature as part of the plan. The relevance of these is explored later.

## Stage 2: areas of experience

This stage of planning involves examining the range of experiences which can be offered to pupils. The Programmes of Study need to be translated into classroom activities. Before considering each of the three areas for science, the ways in which some other classroom activities can contribute to the scientific curriculum are explored.

### Sand and water play

Children need handling experiences to explore these media before attempting to work systematically on activities. An example of this can be seen in groups exploring floating and sinking (Programmes of Study for Key Stage 1, Science Attainment Target 4) when they have not had sufficient opportunities to play with and splash about in a water tray. Extending the range of experiences offered in play activities can include the addition of items not designed for that use.

Water trays can be supplemented by the use of:

- cardboard boxes and paper bags;
- a variety of gloves (wool, cotton, leather, rubber etc.);
- food colourings (drop in and allow children to mix);
- hypo-allergic soaps and washing-up liquids;
- warm water and ice cubes.

Sand Trays can be used with:

- sieves, colanders, flour sifters and tea strainers;
- a variety of small bags made out of cloth with different sizes of holes in;
- wet and dry sand;
- sand and soil mixtures.

### Songs and music

Music Lessons, especially music-making sessions, are often the best time to allow pupils to 'experience a range of sounds' (Programmes of Study for Science, Attainment Target 4). The introduction of a wide variety of objects to hit can enhance the range of sounds. Screw-topped bottles can be used to fill with different objects for shaking – remember to include things such as rice which make soft sounds and cotton wool which fails to produce any sound. A very popular if somewhat noisy activity involves stringing a 'washing line' across the classroom for the children to hang a variety of objects from. The hanging collection (from metal pans, lengths of piping, coke cans to dowel rods), is hit and shaken to explore possible sound effects.

## Home corner

Scientific activities can often emphasise a degree of sharing. Children who have had opportunities to play in communal areas are more likely to work happily alongside or with other children. A variety of materials can be provided for handling opportunities such as metal, paper and wooden dishes and plates, thick and thin plastic, cloth and paper table cloths and changing floor coverings. Early opportunities for organising themselves in groups can be provided through tasks such as setting the table for themselves and one guest.

## Art and craft

Children can mix their own colours using powder and liquid paints. Handling experiences can include chalk, pastels, paints, crayons, glues and pens on a variety of surfaces (e.g. tissue, blotting, sugar, cartridge and greaseproof papers). Many artistic activities, such as dripping marbling inks onto a tray of water, can stimulate excitement and curiosity, encouraging children to want to 'find out' which is the first stage of acquiring skills. Children can explore changes in different materials, such as plaster of paris and self-hardening clay.

## Cookery

Considering the type of cooking children currently experience raises questions of how relevant are activities such as the production of trays of identical cakes. Extending these experiences might involve the added dimension of keeping one cake uncooked to compare to the cooked cakes and including a wider variety of foods. Investigations can include finding out what happens if you add too much or too little water or mashed potato powders, how much water different pastas absorb in cooking, using different whisks to make milk shakes and tasting different jellies (do all ed jellies taste the same?) Associated activities could include finding out what happens if you use metal, wooden or plastic spoons to stir hot liquids or testing different ways of cleaning kitchen surface.

**Key Stage 1**

The following section contains a summary of the Programmes of Study requirements for Key Stage 1 for each of the three areas of scientific knowledge and understanding together with examples of suitable activities. The examples are designed to show how each activity can have a variety of outcomes. They reflect only a very small sample of the many activities which can be planned in this way.

*A. Living things*

Pupils should have opportunities to observe a wide variety of living things. They should help to care for living things and find out about their needs. Pupils should find out about themselves, their needs and the differences between themselves and other pupils. They should consider how to keep themselves healthy and identify parts of their bodies and stages of human development. They should identify parts of plants and be aware of new and extinct life. Local habitats should be studied featuring changes in the local environment and effects of waste disposal.

There are many possible activities on which the study of living things can be based. Pupils can explore the school grounds or a local park observing living things. Some children can tear or cut up leaf shapes and take these to compare to those of plants they find. Other children can use reference books to identify species and make their own charts or keys of the plants they find. Weeds can be dug up whole and some children can sort the different parts, (leaves, roots, stem and flowers), into sets whilst others make close observational drawings and measurements of leaf area. Growing tests can include simple explorations of what happens to seeds grown in the dark to controlled investigations to show the effects of different types of pollution on plant growth. Children exploring waste materials can start by looking at the variety of 'rubbish' left behind after a family breakfast (orange juice carton, cereal box, crusts of bread, fruit peel, and tea bags etc.). For some children, exploring decay will need to have the time factor removed. Activities such as sorting a collection of old and new objects will lead to a discussion of how you can tell if something is old or new and then to identifying evidence of decay. Other children will be able to bury objects in a garden for a period and use photographs to compare what they look like when dug up and before burying.

*B. Materials*

Pupils should compare different materials and their properties and uses. They should explore how these materials can be changed, especially by simple processes including heating and cooling. They should observe the natural environment, including rocks, soil and weathering. They should consider seasonal weather changes and how these affect our lives.

Children can explore a variety of materials. Their own clothing or packaging are good starting points. Comparing packets will involve some children examining size to see if they will fit inside each other and how much they will hold and testing to find which can hold water, flour and biscuits. Other children will be able to plan and carry out investigations to compare the strength of different shapes, suitability for use and properties such as waterproofing. Collections of materials can be compared for feel (e.g. hide some of one material in a bag; can you feel which one it is?) whilst other children find ways to describe similarities and differences between them. Baked potatoes, ice cubes and slices of bread can be used to compare properties of insulation and keeping things fresh with some children wrapping them in different materials and others planning and carrying out a fair test.

A class comparing soil samples could have groups working on sorting the parts of the soil (stones, plant debris, small creatures, etc.), investigating how quickly each sample absorbs water and which creates the best growing environment.

Suitcases can be packed with selections of clothing for different weather conditions for children to compare to seasons (e.g. which case is packed for a winter holiday?) Children working towards a higher level can compare their coats and plan a test to show which types of material are warmest for a winter coat. Children keeping daily weather records can have groups noting their observations on a chart to which others add temperature and accurate rainfall readings.

## C. Forces and energy

Pupils should explore how pushes and pulls can make things move, speed up, stop and change shape. They should find out how different toys move and explore objects which float and sink. They should know that some things use electricity and that they can be dangerous. They should use batteries, buzzers, bulbs and magnets. Pupils should investigate the fuels used at home and school. They should explore ways of making sounds and light and experience sorting colours, hearing echoes, and making shadows and reflections. They should be aware of seasonal changes in the local environment and changes in day length, the sun's position and the moon's appearance.

Collections of things which will and will not roll can be sorted into sets. The activity can be extended by challenging the more able children to find ways of stopping the rollers rolling, or making the non-rollers roll, (ideas usually include adding plasticine or sticking paper plates on the end of square boxes). Ways of making things roll further or faster can be explored (e.g. down slopes or on different surfaces). Coloured rollers can be made by filling clear plastic bottles with small coloured objects (e.g. aquarium gravel, water and glitter, coloured water and baby oil or beads) or painting the outside. Noisy rollers can be made by putting in stones, nails or small bells. Coloured and noisy rollers are especially useful for focussing attention on the object as it rolls.

Pupils can play with toys which move in a variety of ways and make them move on different surfaces along a smooth floor and the playground and through water and air. Boats with sails in the water tray and paper fish shapes on a smooth floor can be used to find different ways of making 'winds' to move them. Moving tools such as hand whisks, or drills can be used with spinners and toy windmills to investigate turning things. Pupils can use magnets to explore what they can and cannot pick up. More able children can be introduced to using Newton Meters to measure force by pulling cars up ramps, shoes along different surfaces and boats across water trays whilst other children may need to play with toy cars on the different surfaces.

Children can sort collections of household items into those which use and those which do not use electricity. Some children can reinforce this by cutting and pasting catalogue pictures whilst others can make lists of appliances used in the home and at school. Torches can be switched on and off and made to work (to make this activity more challenging for some children provide some torches where the batteries need changing, putting in or are in the wrong way round). Children can be given an open circuit to see what happens when they complete it. Different materials can be used to bridge the gap and find which do and do not light the bulb. Some children can use coloured materials to find ways of making coloured lights whilst others make simple switches and find ways of controlling the flow of electricity (e.g. using a cut open graphite pencil to make a dimmer switch).

Light patterns can be made by moving torches around in articles with holes in such as sieves and colanders. Mirrors and torches can be used together to explore reflections. Some children can explore patterns made whilst others systematically investigate the relationship between the direction of the beam to the mirror and the angle of reflection. Games can be played to identify and explore shadows. Pupils can see what happens to their shadows when they move; make their own shadow only have one leg; work with a friend to make a two-headed shadow, and make simple shadow puppets using torn or cut shapes stuck onto thin sticks (these can be moved towards and away from a light source). Children can mark where shadows are at different times of day and make shadow clocks. Shakers can be made with different fillings (including some which do not produce sounds) in plastic jars or bottles with screw tops. Pupils can go on 'sound walks' using a tape to record the different sounds heard. More able children can find out which sounds carry best over a distance and plan and carry out sound proofing investigations.

Many scientific activities carried out in classrooms have explored single ideas so that children considering sounds have handled collections which all make loud sounds and nothing which appears silent. Special Needs Pupils especially require experiences which offer contrasting ideas so that exploring light should include experiencing being in the dark, transparent objects compared to non-transparent and strong tastes matched to things with comparatively little taste (e.g. strong orange squash and water). Some children will quickly need extension activities whilst others require 'more of the same'. In this way children who have been looking through a collection of materials to see which they can see through may need to shine torches through the objects, cover sun glasses frames with different materials and put coloured objects into the container to see which are clearly seen, which change colour and which cannot be seen. Teachers will find the examples used in the National Curriculum Orders useful when considering ways of extending the basic activities for more able pupils. Many Primary Science Schemes, such as Collins Primary Science, offer complementary Key Stage 1 and 2 activities.

**Stage 3: detailed planning**

When planning an individual or a series of classroom activities teachers will need to consider the range of abilities within the group. The case study given here shows how one teacher met the needs of different children within the class and how the children were involved in the classroom as a learning environment. The class of seven year olds were working on an environmental project and had been considering recycling and waste disposal. The teacher took part of the Programme of Study for Key Stage 2; 'investigate the key factors in the process of decay such as temperature, moisture, air and the role of microbes'. The range of abilities in the class meant that the work needed to be planned at three levels:

(a) activities for children still working within level 1;
(b) activities for children who were ready for level 3;
(c) activities for children who were capable of level 4 and possibly might achieve level 5.

The teacher started by encouraging all children to consider the variety of waste produced by a household.

GROUP A – had a breakfast table set up in the home corner. They were encouraged to discuss which items would be used again and which would be thrown away. They then sorted the rubbish into cardboard, plastic, food items etc.

GROUP B – put on rubber gloves and went on a 'scavenger hunt' around the school. They sorted their collection into items which they thought would rot and those things which would not. They were encouraged to give reasons for how they classified the collection.

GROUP C – started by listing the types of rubbish they thought their families produced and sorting into items which could be re-cycled and those which could not. They wrote to the Local Council to ask what happened to the different types of rubbish and found information about can re-cycling and bottle banks. The teacher wanted the children to consider the effects of decay on different materials.

GROUP A – played the 'Old Mother Hubbard' game where they had a collection of old and new things from the cupboard (shiny and rusty tins, fresh and shrivelled apples, fresh and dry bread, new and scratched plastic bowls etc.). They put on rubber gloves and quickly sorted the collection into old and new sets. They were then asked to say how they knew which sets to put things in and each child took a pair of items and drew each one with key words around it.

GROUP B – made collections of items which they thought would and would not rot. They took photographs and made drawings of each thing. They made labels with permanent markers on lolly sticks and buried their items in the school grounds. They discussed how long to leave them before digging them up and used a word processor to write what they hoped to find out.

GROUP C – worked to plan a group investigation to find out about which factors accelerated decay. They chose two areas; some thought that how wet things were was significant whilst others decided to find out if wrapping things in different materials would stop decay. They decided to work in two groups but with each group using the same items. They chose apples, bread and potatoes and each group planned how to carry out their investigation. The first group decided to use the same amount of each item and to put the items in plastic egg boxes with different amounts of water (measured by a pipette). They put all their boxes, covered with cling film, on the same window sill and elected to make daily observations. The second group choose a variety of materials (from cling film to tissue paper) and wrapped the same size samples in each. They left one sample of each item unwrapped and put all their samples in a dark cupboard agreeing to leave them for one week before unwrapping.

The work continued in the same way with children working at appropriate levels but being aware of and sharing other groups' activities.

## Conclusion

Many children with special needs have been denied a full, balanced curriculum. Scientific activities can offer varied experiences which contribute to the development of the whole child and allow easily targeted

28

successes. The National Curriculum has offered an opportunity to re-examine the types of activity which can be offered to extend learning opportunities and the science curriculum can be used to provide pupils with an increased understanding of the world they live in.

## References and further reading

Harlen, W., Macro, C., Shilling, M., Malvern, D., and Reed, K. (1990) *Progress in Primary Science*. Routledge: London.

Howe, L. (1990) *Collins Primary Science*. Harper Collins: London.

NCC, (1992) *Forces – a Guide for Teachers*. National Curriculum Council: York.

NCC, (1991) *Science Explorations*. National Curriculum Council: York.

NCC, (1992) *Teaching Science to Pupils with Special Educational Needs*. National Curriculum Council: York.

Novak, J. D. and Gowin, D. R. (1984) *Learning How to Learn*. Cambridge University Press: Cambridge.

Richards R., Collins, M. and Kincaid D. (1987) *An Early Start to Science. Macdonald: London.*

*Kincaid, D., Rapson, H. and Richards, R. (1983) Science for Children with Learning Difficulties.* (Learning Through Science Series), Macdonald Educational: London.

# CHAPTER 2

# *Mathematics in Transition*

*Alec Williams*

## Traditional practice in special education

The notion that the curriculum in special education should be rigorously assessed and evaluated against normal curriculum practice in mainstream schools is of relatively recent origin.

The Warnock Report (DES, 1978), Brennan (1979) and Wilson (1981) represented the first major challenges to curriculum practices that had characterised special education from the time it had begun to expand rapidly in the post-war period. Previously it had been assumed that the overriding factor in deciding curricular priorities should be the perceptions of the school, and of the individual teacher, of the social, personal and vocational needs of young persons who would be vulnerable in adjusting to the challenge of the outside world. Insights gained through continuing post-school contacts, often substantiated by follow-up dissertation studies, influenced the form and substance of much of the curriculum, particularly in special schools.

At best, outward-looking and imaginative programmes were developed, well attuned to the goals of social and vocational adjustment, within what Brennan (1979) had termed an 'adaptive' curriculum. Many were the sources and inspiration for 'lifeskills' programmes adopted in local mainstream schools. Subsequently, they made a major contribution to the Technical and Vocational Education Initiative (TVEI), the Certificate of Pre-vocational Education (CPVE), the Youth Training Scheme (YTS) and similar initiatives.

In such a frame of reference, mathematics could be expected to focus tightly on the four basic processes and how to apply them, on calculations and the management of money and time and on everyday practical measurements. In the pursuit of such objectives teachers tended to produce a variety of card assignments, often related to the realities of the neighbourhood of the school. These could be supplemented by an impressive range of published books and materials with comparable aims. In special schools, 'leavers' programmes' set realistic mathematical challenges, both within the community itself and with simulation projects within the school.

During this lengthy period, contact and interaction between special and mathematical educators was minimal. Many of the special needs Diploma courses bore little effective content related to mathematics. What scant literature did exist, seeking to relate the respective disciplines, almost invariably had its origins in contemporary special school practice and thus sought to refine rather than challenge existing thinking.

It should therefore occasion little surprise that challenges to the established order came not from special education but from the mathematicians. The Cockcroft Report (DES, 1982) offered for non-academic pupils a 'Foundation List', a widely-discussed and imaginative programme offering calculators, graphical representation, ratio and proportion and a 'critical attitude to statistics presented by the media', all within a context of realism and relevance. The Schools Council project 'Low Attainers in Mathematics 5-16' (Denvir *et al.*, 1982) presented a critical review and evaluation of existing practice. It established links between professionals from both disciplines, engendering a climate in which the Mathematical Association and the National Association for Remedial Education jointly established and validated a Diploma course linking mathematics and special education for teachers in secondary schools. The process of change was undoubtedly given added momentum by the coincidental timing of these two major reports.

### The National Curriculum and mathematics

That neither the original Task Group on Attainment and Testing (TGAT), nor the subsequent working groups in the core subjects included anyone representing special education was a matter for deep concern. Was special education yet again to be accorded only 'bolt-on' status in a national education reform?

The proposals for mathematics in the first consultation document (NCC, 1988a) unacceptably attempted to link listed disabilities to types of learning difficulties. Of greater significance was the unequivocal statement that ' . . . as far as possible children with special educational needs should remain within the mainstream framework of attainment targets and programmes of study'. *Struggle* (1989), a journal devoted solely to mathematics within special education, presented a digest of responses to the consultation document from professional bodies representing both mathematics and special education. All respondents favoured the inclusion of every pupil in the National Curriculum with minimal uses of disapplication procedures. Recent evidence of a unanimous acceptance of this principle is to be found in a report by H.M.I. visiting twenty-six ordinary and fifty special schools (DES, 1991). It is reported that:

> ... none was proposing to disapply any part of the curriculum for any pupil with statements.

What motives have prompted such a reaction from special education to proposals for a curriculum that appears to challenge existing beliefs and practices to such a degree? How far can acceptance be explained by a conviction that the National Curriculum in mathematics is worth-while in its own right for pupils with special educational needs? Or is it a determination that, come what may, those pupils are to be spared the stigma that is likely to be associated with exclusion procedures? The gains in acceptance achieved through the Warnock Report and the 1981 Education Act are obviously not being ceded lightly!

### Profile Component 3: applications, personal qualities and language

Predictably, the *Struggle* report gave unreserved support to the working group's proposal that Profile Component 3 should be devoted entirely to the application of mathematical skills, to personal qualities and to the language of mathematics, with a weighting of 40:30:30 in favour of Profile Component 3 to give added significance to these dimensions of mathematical behaviour. Eighty per cent of respondents shared the view that their significance would be threatened if they were to be incorporated into the other profile components. Nevertheless, three months later, the Consultation Report (NCC, 1988b) had dispensed with this component entirely.

*Applications* were demoted to the status of separate attainment targets within Profile Components 1 and 2, thus tempting a conclusion that the acquisition of skills, knowledge and concepts in mathematics should be practised and assessed independently of their use and application! In the most recent Draft Order for mathematics (NCC, 1991a) the separation of the New Attainment Target 1 still serves to represent application skills as products rather than as an integral part of the processes embodied in the development of mathematical skills and concepts. The editors of *Struggle* (1989) had already complained:

> To bury this component (application) as the Secretaries of State have done is to ignore what has been learnt about the transfer of skills and to disregard the complaints of employers who are not interested in the theoretical achievements of their young employees but in those who are able to apply their skills to any problem they may meet.

Larcombe (1988) discusses the possibility that pupils who can remember techniques but not apply them to real problems could be unduly rewarded in an assessment system lacking Profile Component 3. Fortunately, ambiguities regarding the significance of application skills have been less apparent in subsequent publications. The well-received *Mathematics: Non-Statutory Guidance* (NCC, 1989a) makes use of heavy print only once throughout its length to emphasise:

> The National Curriculum requires all schools to develop a teaching and learning approach in which the uses and applications of mathematics permeate and influence all work in mathematics.

In one quarter at least, Profile Component 3 lives on!

*Personal Qualities* have not reappeared as attainment targets following the stated conclusions that they were neither specific to mathematics and nor were they susceptible to practical forms of measurement. Larcombe (1988) challenged their inclusion mainly on the grounds of the dubious validity of postulating specific personal qualities as invariant attributes of successful mathematical behaviour. That the National Curriculum is thus now exclusively content-based can in no way devalue, for the teacher in special education, its traditional and deeply-felt concern with the ideational and attitudinal priorities in the teaching and learning of mathematics. Five of the ten stated aims in the teaching of mathematics proposed in *Mathematics from 5–16* (DES, 1985) relate directly to personal qualities and have lost nothing in importance:

- an awareness of the fascination of mathematics;
- imagination, initiative and flexibility of mind;
- working in an independent way;
- working co-operatively;
- confidence in own mathematical ability.

A similar view may be taken of the withdrawal of the specific *language* element, discarded in the Consultative Report on grounds of inexpediency for formal assessment, with the added comment that communication skills could await (later) cross-curricular attention. The apparent under-valuing of the primacy of the language factor will not impress teachers in special education who have learned from experience that language disabilities are a major factor inhibiting progress in mathematical learning. Incidental acquisition of both receptive and expressive mathematical vocabularies is unlikely for a substantial minority of pupils for whom systematic programming is essential. From teachers so engaged, the words of Cockcroft (1982) will receive unqualified support:

> In their learning, children need to develop their understanding of words and expressions through discussions and activities and this development of mathematical language must continue through all stages as an integral part of the curriculum.

The Mathematical Association's *Maths Talk* (1990), drawing upon the Bullock Report's 'eleven uses of language' (1975), is required reading for the teacher in special education seeking a well-argued exposition of the place of language in the teaching of mathematics along with an abundance of advice and ideas for practical classroom usage.

## A curriculum for all?

Regretfully, the non-statutory guidance document for mathematics contains no reference to pupils with special educational needs. The Special Educational Needs Task Group, chaired by Dr Ronald Davie, was established too late to inform and influence any of the non-statutory guidance documents in the core subjects. The task group's *A Curriculum for All* (NCC, 1989b) was thus obliged to serve as a form of supplement to the mathematics document. Efforts to dissuade mainstream colleagues of the existence of a cut-off point at which education becomes 'special', in favour of the concept of a continuum of ability and need are not enhanced by the necessity for a separate publication.

Nevertheless *A Curriculum for All* represents, in its own right, a milestone in curriculum development in special education. Its opening statement affirms the right of every pupil to a broad and balanced curriculum, taking due account of the differential needs of the individual child. It draws upon the best in contemporary practice in special and mainstream schools, presenting well formulated ideas and ideals within a fundamentally dynamic and optimistic framework.

Inevitably there are omissions and shortcomings; the apparently insuperable problems of how to translate the new challenges and aspirations into practice. The seemingly hopelessly wide attainment target demands, the changes and confusion regarding assessment, the dilemma of quality versus breadth and the intricacies associated with differentiation – all merit treatment at a depth that the document cannot offer. Optimism as to the pupils' abilities to achieve within the wide curricular demands is matched by aspirations as to the quality of learning to be achieved:

> Like their peers, pupils with special educational needs should be involved in tasks which encourage making predictions, solving problems, carrying out investigations and testing hypotheses.

The teacher striving to achieve understandings with pupils of very limited ability may react to such a statement without enthusiasm – the credibility gap between his/her reality situation and the aims as presented may be regarded as too wide to offer either guidance or inspiration. Or does such a response bear out the oft-repeated assertion that pupils with special educational needs are too frequently under-challenged and under-functioning?

## Width and depth in the National Curriculum

Is determination to ensure right of access to the National Curriculum less than realistic for numbers of pupils whose teachers are nevertheless determined that that right shall be exercised? The complexities and rate of change in today's society are such that more and better informed decisions are asked of its citizens in every walk of life. A National Curriculum seeking to prepare pupils for responsible participation in such a society can do no other than to match its demands in both width and depth. The problem for the teacher of pupils with special educational needs is to attempt to reconcile the range and complexity of such demands with the needs and abilities of pupils for whom learning can be a slow, difficult and frustrating process and who make progress only when given more time, more reinforcement, more examples on which to draw and frequently, more individualised forms of intervention. In mathematics, the introduction of five 'New' attainment targets to replace the previous fourteen (NCC, 1991b), represents an item reshuffle rather than any alleviation of demand.

Particular problems are associated with Level 1 where:

> ...attainment targets represent, for a wide range of pupils with special educational needs, levels of challenge which are likely to be achieved only by the setting of intermediate goals with a need for encouragement and support, careful pacing of work and activities which are both finely graded developmentally and appropriately age-related. *A Curriculum for All* (NCC, 1989b).

Where such strategies are appropriate, time must be found to make meticulous checks on understanding and ability to transfer gained from behaviourally devised programmes which can present discrete objectives with little guarantee that the learning can be generalised. Quality teaching of this order calls for sensitivity, selectivity and differentiation.

### *Selectivity and differentiation*

Given the foregoing, within the National Curriculum teachers have a responsibility to decide which attainment targets and associated programmes of study should be accorded priority – but against what criteria?

The National Curriculum does not discriminate in this way. It places an obligation on teachers to give attention to every attainment target. To query this dictum is to challenge the principles on which the National Curriculum has been conceived. Yet to apply it literally would be to deny the special nature of those needs. *A Cuuriculum for All* qualifies its appeal for breadth by reference to the necessity for balance, relevance and differentiation:

> Detailed knowledge of the mathematical profiles of individual pupils which has been acquired by the teacher through discussion, observation and supportive intervention will suggest the most appropriate teaching strategies.

Profile awareness can contribute to, though not in itself determine, subsequent curricular decisions regarding direction, depth and pace for the individual pupil. The necessity for balance between the demands of the National Curriculum and the teacher's interpretation of personal need will require avoidance at one extreme of pupils confused and frustrated by inappropriate demands or, alternately, denial of access to opportunities for achievement and fulfilment within a wider curriculum.

Spurred by the National Curriculum, imagination and ingenuity are being exercised by teachers in planning and directing activities permitting pupils with special educational needs to explore and experience success within hitherto untried areas of the curriculum. Three major factors underlying such success can be identified in this extract from the H.M.I. Report (DES, 1991):

> High standards of work were evident where the teaching expertise involved a combination of knowledge of both the curriculum area and of the particular features of pupils' special needs, together with realistically high expectations of pupil performance.

The prominence currently accorded to the differentiation concept is arguably one of the most significant benefits to accompany the introduction of the National Curriculum. A wide-ranging concept, it covers not only concern for levels of ability but extends to both teaching and individual learning styles, background experience, interests, expectations and forms of motivation (Barthorpe and Visser, 1991). Thus, profiles which indicate similar levels of attainment do not imply a common content to the curriculum. In a class hobbies project for instance, each form of mathematics thrown up by dressmaking and carpentry (estimation and measurement) swimming and athletic track event times (decimals), the designing of a pigeon loft (estimation, planning and costing) and go-cart racing (time, distance and speed) has its value. All are likely to help enrich the quality of life for the individuals concerned and evoke challenges at levels unlikely to be equalled by a single, teacher-determined task.

Such differentiation has its foundation in a respect for the pupil's individuality, the valuing of differences in intention and outcome and, when significant decisions are to be made, recognition of rights to negotiation. For the young or immature pupil, perhaps already inured to failure and frustration, such principles are no less important as a means towards the achievement of personal growth involving confidence, satisfaction and self-respect. Happily, mathematics, both in process and content, provides a wealth of opportunity to advance towards such realisation.

*Differentiation in depth*

In practice, consciously or otherwise, decisions are constantly being taken about the depth to which a skill, topic or concept is to be pursued. Brennan (1979) distinguishes between 'insightful' and 'awareness' learning, the terms representing the extremes of a continuum indicating the quality and degree of understanding and conceptualisation in the learning acquired by the pupil. In the areas of skill acquisition he postulates a comparable 'mastery'/'familiarity' continuum. These notions have a particular significance in mathematics where learning which is insightful and mastered to the level of the pupil's ability to explain, transfer, estimate or predict, (i.e. to the level of *usability*), though essential in key topics and skills, may be neither possible nor necessary for the pupil with special educational needs in relation to less important topics and skills. Brennan continues:

> ... by making deliberate use of the concepts of awareness and familiarity learning, the teacher may plan for the achievement of curricular objectives which allow the pupil to relate and adjust to aspects of his environment which, though not fully understood, extend the pupil's awareness of his membership of society and extend the possibility of areas of the curriculum common to all pupils (Brennan, 1979).

It cannot be stressed too strongly that awareness learning, related to the individual pupil's needs and abilities, is no less important than that which is based on full understanding. Within a common topic, according to pupils' needs and abilities, the appropriate depth of learning is likely to vary from group to group and from individual to individual within the group. This makes heavy demands upon the teaching and class management skills of the teacher. However, the balance achieved by placing the skills and topics on an understanding/awareness continuum can avoid, for both pupil and teacher, the frustration of misplaced effort. It permits time and energy to be used to maximum effect.

*Differentiation and age-expectation*

In an early and considered response to the 1988 consultation document in mathematics, Larcombe (1988) drew attention to both the perils and the opportunities implicit in the National Curriculum system of assessment by Levels. The crucial question for the individual, he suggests, lies not in age-related norms which may come to be popularly associated with the National Curriculum levels, but the Level at which a high degree of success can be demonstrated. The continuum represented by the progressive levels of the programmes of study, carries an implication of a parallel continuum of abilities in relation to pupils.

The responses of the national press, however, to the results of the first Key Stage 1 testing (which, predictably, approximated to a normal curve of distribution) combined concern with degrees of outrage that a seven year level expectation was not being universally met. Under the headline '...seven year failings' the Guardian (28.10.91), complained that 'Fewer than one child in seven could do simple multiplication such as five times five'. Whether $5 \times 5$ is a desirable attainment for seven year-olds is beside the point. Shifting attainments to different National Curriculum levels would be unlikely to modify popular reaction to the new expectancies. The Cockcroft Report (1982) postulated a seven year spread of ability in mathematics at eleven years. With the widening spread of mathematical attainment in the later years of secondary schooling, a still more vociferous press reaction can confidently be predicted when the outcomes of testing at Key Stages 3 and 4 are made known.

Age-expectancy is not of course confined to the press. How far is the serious confusion experienced by many pupils in relation to place value explained by its virtually universal introduction prior to pupil transfer to junior school? At this age a substantial minority is expected to master this most vital yet abstract of concepts when developmentally they have yet to grasp even the basic notion of the permanence of quantities (conservation of number; New Attainment Target 1, Level 1). Subsequent expactancies, implicit in whole-class teaching methods, are commonly to be found in the teaching of mathematics, particularly within the secondary school. Careful attention on the part of the individual teacher to the differential variables hitherto considered in this chapter, can be brought to nought by a school, a system or a society that persists in disregarding developmental realities.

## Relevance and motivation

All pupils, including those with special educational needs, are usually more motivated and derive more enjoyment from mathematics when it has obvious personal meaning for them. *A Curriculum for All* (DES, 1989b).

Though neither breadth nor balance could fairly be considered characteristic of the traditional mathematics curriculum in special education, a claim to relevance may appear more assured. Travelling, timekeeping, punctuality, purchasing, credit, saving and budgetting were common to most adaptive programmes. They were relevant, undeniably in the quest for socially adaptive skills, but claims to their oft-quoted motiv- ation and enjoyment merit further consideration. For the pupil whose employment prospects are bleak, time devoted to the mathematical intricacies and abstractions of the wage-deduction slip is unlikely to be regarded as satisfying, or even relevant. For many pupils, purpose in mathematics related to the long-term future rather than immediate concerns and with no element of personal choice is likely to evoke a flat response. Clocking-in and out practices, simulated hire-purchase agreements and the like, though having some claim to attention, can never substitute for the involvement in and the commitment of the pupil to problems arising of his or her own making or derived from the collective need of a group activity.

Mathematics so derived is likely to engender confidence, high motivation and an ability to identify and deal mathematically with real situations that can subsequently be generalised and applied to many of the important but mundane survival skills required in later life. *Mathematics; Non-Statutory guidance* (NCC, 1989a), stressing the importance of giving thought to '. . . identifying the opportunities that exist for developing mathematics out of cross-curricular work', comments that this can be achieved'. . . through the pupil's *own* (writer's italics) experiences in the life of the school'.

*Why only across the curriculum?*

> The world in which pupils live is not compartmentalised into subjects. Their curiosity, questions and ways of thinking transcend subject barriers. *A Curriculum for All* (DES, 1989b).

The notion that mathematics can enrich and be enriched by its application in other subjects has few challengers. Conceptualisation is enhanced by exploiting opportunities for re-using existing skills and, where feasible, extending them as the situation permits. Admirably, National Curriculum documentation abounds with advice and exhortation in this respect. Much less attention however is devoted to the opportunities for exploiting situations for mathematical purposes in activities lying outside the formal subject areas where an infinitely wide range of opportunities can generate powerful motivational drives unknown in teacher-directed classroom practice. Pupils' acceptance of the mathematical responsibilities implicit in outings and visits, by whatever means of transport, can undoubtedly involve the odd hazard but when positively tackled by the teacher, few mistakes are repeated. Shielding pupils from decision-making is a doubtful preparation for later life.

A residential special school successfully delegated to its senior pupils responsibility for all aspects of financing its much-used minibus and subsequently went on systematically to identify and exploit the mathematical opportunities in its varied day-to-day usage. A more economically and less casually used vehicle was the outcome. Other challenges recently accepted have included the mathematics of a sponsored walk (13 year-old M.L.Ds), planning and running the class Christmas party (top juniors; 'Can we do it again ourselves next time?') and devising and running sideshows at a charity bazaar (mixed-ability 14 year-olds). Compared with such activities, class simulations devised as vehicles for mathematical applications, can appear to the pupil trivial and contrived. Excitingly, once the tradition of exploiting genuine events for their mathematical opportunities has been established, the pupils themselves tend to identify the activities involving mathematical potentialities, both in and out of the classroom.

**Control and freedom in the use of mathematics**

The advent of the National Curriculum has brought to the fore the problems regarding the degree of teacher control and intervention in practical activities involving mathematics. How far should the spontaneity which has characterised so much of the practical and project work in special education be sacrificed so that achievements can be related to and monitored against National Curriculum targets? Is it possible that the apparent constraints so imposed may be in the pupils' interests? Unlike the controlled and essentially 'tidy' problems presented by the teacher and the textbook, real-life mathematics can arise unexpectedly, may include extraneous and unexpected elements, may be in a confusing or unfamiliar context, may lend itself to several 'answers' and require recourse to skills as yet un-covered in the classroom. Whilst decision-making and adaptability are prime objectives in adopting this approach, a modicum of pre-planning can pre-empt individual difficulties and also help to achieve the ordered progression implicit in the National Curriculum structures. To this end the maintenance of the class mathematics records in a simple matrix form will be found to facilitate an at-a-glance appraisal of abilities of class, group and individuals in respect of the skills, concepts and knowledge involved. The availability of such a record, both at the pre-planning and subsequent stages when critical decisions are called for, permits the balance between flexibility and control to be maintained.

*Readiness for problem solving*

Participation in activities involving investigating, formulating arguments, considering alternatives, reaching decisions and accepting associated responsibilities is dependent upon levels of confidence and personal maturity as much as mathematical abilities. Pupils whose mathematical horizons have been limited to texts and worksheets cannot be exposed to the full rigours of open-ended, interactive challenges in mathematics without preparation.

Larcombe (1985), in suggesting a graduated programme of 'fore-runners', sees the growth of confidence as a prerequisite to success in active project work. He recommends that pupils begin with activities requiring a 'do' or 'say' response, planned to ensure 100 per cent success, leading on to guessing games, drawing, at this stage, on their sensory perceptions rather than challenging their thinking skills. Double, and then multiple-choice problems precede the ultimate challenge of open-ended enquiries; all in a supportive, non-critical climate where the most hesitant contributions are encouraged and valued. Colleagues in mathematical education would have us believe that it is delight in the subject for its own sake that is the subject's prime motivation. Pupils with special educational needs who experience mathematical growth through participation in active problem-solving provide encouraging evidence that intrinsic satisfaction of this order need not be denied them.

## Personal formulation of mathematics

> It is often assumed that techniques must be learned and practised before problems are mentioned. This can lead to mis-understanding and lack of meaning. When pupils complain that they 'did not see the point of doing all these', they are given a remote justification, 'You'll need it when you buy a carpet,' *Better Mathematics* (Ahmed, 1987).

Even today, many published texts in mathematics tend to perpetuate presentations whereby context-free mechanical exercises precede analagous problems. The latter are likely to be predictable as to the process(es) involved and most unlikely to include the unplanned extraneous elements characteristic of real-life situations. Thus, the opportunities for pupils to learn to recognise the mathematics in an everyday situation and to abstract and process the relevant data from it are rarely experienced if the ready-made and reality-free formulations of the textbook have been the main component of their mathematical diet. Hart's Chelsea College studies (1981) confirmed – disturbingly – that many pupils who had mastered the four basic processes in mathematics were unable to identify in simple multiple-choice tests, which of them to use for solving simple everyday problems. Thus is presented another 'balance' for the teacher to strive to attain – that between the use of textbooks and involvement in the mathematics of reality.

From the earliest stages, pupils need opportunities to join in practical activities which, with teacher's help, they can recognise as being relevant to mathematical skills which are going to be taught and practised. If the balance is achieved, the pupil learns to relate one area of experience to another, not only enhancing the ability to formulate personal mathematics but to generalise and extend that which has been learned.

## Following the transition . . .

In retrospect it can be argued that regardless of the advent of the National Curriculum, a serious challenge to much of the mathematical inertia that often characterised past practice in special education was long overdue. The case for the retention of traditional practice in maintaining a restricted 'adaptive' curriculum in mathematics on grounds of social and vocational adaptiveness had already been challenged by Brennan (1979):

> . . . at what point does that differentiation become a separatist device in that it cuts off the slow learner from the common aspects of the curriculum which contribute to cultural and social cohesion in our society?

Let it be assumed that the argument in favour of greater breadth in the mathematics curriculum for pupils with special educational needs is accepted. This chapter has put the case that for the teacher, the decisions to be made relate not only to selection of content and the manner of its teaching but also, of no less importance, to the depth to which that content is to be taken.

The provision of wider opportunities in areas hitherto unsought and unrecognised presents an unprecedented challenge but also throws wide open the question as to the aims and objectives of teaching mathematics to children with special educational needs in the conditions of today. It is vital that the outcomes are rigorously monitored and evaluated so that as and when the form and demands of the National Curriculum in mathematics achieve a relative permanence, the teacher in special education can draw upon both past and new experience in drawing up a personal reformulation of teaching aims and objectives. In this respect, the statement from *Better Mathematics* (Ahmed, 1987), written prior to the advent of the National Curriculum has lost none of its validity:

> Aims can only act as forces for change and development when those who are to use and understand them are actively involved in either their evaluation or in working at their implications as they affect their own situation.

### References

Ahmed, A. (1987) *Better Mathematics*. A Curriculum Development Study based on the Low Attainers in Mathematics project (L.A.M.P.) London: H.M.S.O.

Barthorpe, P. & Visser, J. (1991) *Differentiation: Your Responsibility*. Stafford: N.A.R.E. Publications.

Brennan, W. K. (1979) *Curricular Needs of Slow Learners*. London: Evans/Methuen.

Denvir, B. (*et al.*). (1982) *Low Attainers in Mathematics 5-16*. Schools Council Working Paper No. 72. London: Methuen.

DES, (1975) *A Language for Life* (*Bullock Report*). London: H.M.S.O.

DES, (1978) *Special Educational Needs* (Warnock Report). London: H.M.S.O.

DES, (1982) *Mathematics Counts*. (Cockcroft Report). London: H.M.S.O.

DES, (1985) *Mathematics from 5-16*. London: H.M.S.O.

DES, (1991) *National Curriculum and Special Needs: A Report by H.M. Inspectorate*. London: H.M.S.O.

Hart, K. M. (1981) (Ed). *Children's Understanding of Mathematics*. London: John Murray.

Larcombe. T. (1985) *Mathematical Learning Difficulties in the Secondary School*. Milton Keynes: Open University.

Larcombe, T. (1988) Mathematics: Prospects and Problems. *British Journal of Special Education*. **15**, 4, 163-6.

Mathematical Association (1989) The National Curriculum: Response to 'Mathematics for ages 5-16'. In *Struggle* No. 24.

Mathematical Association (1990) *Maths Talk*. Cheltenham: Stanley Thomas.

National Curriculum Council (Aug. 1988a) *Mathematics for Ages 5-16*. (Consultation document: Proposals) York: N.C.C.

National Curriculum Council (Nov. 1988b) *Mathematics for Ages 5-16*. (Report on responses to consultation document) York: N.C.C.

42

National Curriculum Council (1989a) *Mathematics: Non-Statutory Guidance*. York: N.C.C.

National Curriculum Council (1989b) *A Curriculum for All: Special Educational Needs in the National Curriculum* York: N.C.C.

National Curriculum Council (Aug. 1991a) *Draft Order for Mathematics*. (Proposals for 5 New A.Ts) York: N.C.C.

National Curriculum Council (Oct. 1991b) *Draft Order for Mathematics (Report on responses to consultation document) York: N.C.C.*

*Wilson, M. D. (1981) The Curriculum in Special Schools*. Harlow: Longman.

# CHAPTER 3

# English: Running with a Handicap

*Barrie Wade*

## 1. Introduction

At the outset of this chapter I am much preoccupied with English Attainment Target 3 (Writing) and specifically with statement of attainment 7(d). Readers who also choose to consult my article 'English: half way there' (Wade, 1989) will be able to assess from the following pages whether I successfully:

> demonstrate an increased awareness that a first draft may be changed, amended and reordered . . .' (DES & Welsh Office, 1990, p. 14).

or whether I am still 'working towards' level 7. Other readers will certainly notice that the original positive title has been changed to one indicating deficit that hampers an otherwise potentially fluent performance.

The first report of the National Curriculum English Working Group (DES & Welsh Office, 1988) was a considerable achievement. In a short time the group sifted a mass of evidence, formulated guidelines for policies and specified profile components, attainment targets and programmes of study for pupils aged five to eleven. Work began immediately on the secondary stage and consultation through the National Curriculum Council and the Curriculum Council for Wales proceeded apace to enable the Secretaries of State to place Orders before Parliament and have attainment targets and study programmes for the younger children operating by September, 1989. There was a degree of professional optimism that, if the second report was as rigorous and enlightening as the first, English could really be said to have arrived as a core subject.

The second report of the English Working Group, *English for ages 5 to 16* (DES & Welsh Office, 1989), incorporated the first and, following the Task Group on Assessment and Testing, recommended ten levels of attainment within targets. Meanwhile, however, there had been rumblings of political exasperation. The Secretaries of State, for example, proposed that the first attainment target in writing (see Figure 1) should be changed

> to give greater emphasis to pupils' mastery of the grammatical structure of the English language.

They proposed also that above key stage 1 'reading and writing should be given higher weighting' than speaking and listening. If they had been carried through, these proposals would have had damaging implications for children with special educational needs. They would have devalued oral work for all children and would have led to curriculum imbalance. There are no grounds in logic or linguistics for such emphasis. For many pupils with special educational needs who make slow progress with print such weighting would have been discouraging and positively harmful. In the event, fortunately, there was massive protest about such changes at the consultation stage, so no action was taken.

Although *English for ages 5-16* carefully spelled out coherent policies for teaching about language and for enabling pupils to use language perceptively and effectively in its various modes it became clear that this was not the simple, prescriptive report that Mr. Baker wanted. Nor did it advocate a return to discredited formal grammar teaching as the Secretary of State had hinted it should. Mr. Baker showed his displeasure by printing the English Group's second report in reverse order with chapters 15–17 (attainment targets and study programmes) at the beginning and highlighted on yellow pages. The chairman of the English Working Group, Professor Brian Cox, has since that time made clear how little proper discussion there was with either Mr. Baker or with Mrs. Angela Rumbold, so that it was unclear what parts of the rationale they objected to. In the latter's case:

> it seemed she found repugnant our insistence that a child's dialect is not inaccurate in its use of grammar and should be respected (Cox, 1991, p. 11).

Brian Cox refers also to the way that prejudice sullied the media debate begun by Mr. Baker's insistence on more emphasis on grammar. Contrary to abundant evidence that language varies with purpose, audience and context, some people continued to pretend that there were fixed, simple and unchanging rules governing language use. Some of these people, like Mr. Baker, held high political office. Brian Cox reports that the Prime Minister, Mrs. Thatcher, asked for the necessary qualification 'where appropriate' to be deleted from the Writing statement of attainment 'use Standard English, where appropriate' (Cox, 1991, p. 12).

Thus began the weighting down of the National Curriculum in English with the dross of prejudice and inaccuracy – a handicap which was not apparent in *English for ages 5-11* in 1988. I shall return to the notion of deficit and its causes towards the end of the chapter, but first I will review

| Figure 1 | Profile components, attainment targets and weighting |
|---|---|
| **Profile component** | **Attainment target** |
| 1. Speaking and listening | 1. Pupils should demonstrate their understanding of the spoken word and the capacity to express themselves effectively in a variety of speaking and listening activities, matching style and response to audience and purpose. |
| 2. Reading | 1. The development of the ability to read, understand and respond to all types of writing (70%). 2. The development of reading and information-retrieval and strategies for the purpose of study (30%). |
| 3. Writing | 1. A growing ability to construct and convey meaning in written language (70%). 2. Spelling (20%). 3. Handwriting (10%) |

some of the proposals in the National Curriculum for English by concentrating on this first report of the English Working Group and by considering its potential for teaching English and for the learning of pupils with special educational needs.

## 2. Components, targets and levels

Inevitably the specifying of objectives for 'knowledge, skills, understanding and aptitudes' and a description of 'essential content which needs to be covered' was seen as the main achievement by those politicians who framed the terms of reference. The group recommended three profile components of equal weighting leading to six attainment targets, as Figure 1 shows. Percentages in parentheses show the recommended weighting for various attainment targets within a profile component.

In the second report, *English for ages 5–16*, the two reading attainment targets, as a result of consultation, were merged into one:

> The development of the ability to read, understand and respond to all types of writing, as well as the development of information-retrieval strategies for the purposes of study.

and the spelling and handwriting targets in writing were sensibly merged into a presentation target beyond level 4.

The group carefully specified its intentions regarding attainment targets and these had considerable implications for the education of pupils with special educational needs. First, they clearly stated that 'as far as possible' pupils with special educational needs should 'have the opportunity to experience the full range of the English curriculum' (DES & Welsh Office, 1988, 13.3). Importantly, they defined special educational needs not merely in terms of statemented children. Secondly, the targets in reading, writing, speaking and listening were constructed to 'take heed of the point that development in the four language modes is complex and non-linear' (1.8). Those who had persisted in seeing a child's special needs in language exclusively in terms of reading deficiences were required to think again! Thirdly, the group tried to avoid undesirable washback effects from assessment to classroom practice. Specifically they warned against 'de-contextualised language exercises or other activities of an arid kind' (1.10). It seemed that finally, we were saying goodbye to the days when teachers located in the child problems which, in truth, lay in mindless, unrelated bits of published language activities and the repetitious, boring ways in which these were presented.

Descriptions of original levels of achievement for **Attainment Target 1: Reading** are given in Figure 2 to illustrate the three points made above. Firstly, the descriptions are couched in positive terms of achievement which indicate what pupils should know and be able to do at each level. If the relationship between ages and stages is not insisted upon for pupils with special educational needs, these children should have the chance to show what they *can* do rather than struggling in a system which emphasises what they cannot.

Secondly, reading in the five levels is considered in relation to the other language modes of speaking and listening as well as to pupils' experience. It is through its links with other language modes and with reality that reading becomes a meaningful and pleasurable activity and the child with special educational needs in this area has most need of pleasure and purpose to sustain progress. Curiously, as Figure 2 shows, the group did not originally attempt to make links between writing and reading. Perhaps this was an oversight. Since writing and reading develop profitably together from the earliest stages (see, for example, Payton, 1984) many teachers would wish to make links between them. Important attainments for many pupils with special needs in reading are the abilities to read their own writing and, before that, work they have dictated in their own words which has been transcribed into writing by their teacher or by a fellow-student. However, by the time that Orders were laid before Parliament in March 1990 writing had been incorporated, for example at level 3:

> bring to their writing and discussion about stories some understanding of the way stories are structured

and at level 5:

> demonstrate, in talking and writing about a range of stories and poems which they have read, an ability to explain preferences (DES & Welsh Office, 1990, pp. 8–9).

Thirdly, coherence and continuity were underlined by the emphasis in this attainment target on meaningful stories and poems at all levels. In this way the group built upon what we know about narrative and its relationship (for example, Wade, 1984, p. 8):

Young children and adults use story to organise their experiences and to communicate them to other people. The only difference is that, while adults may also have other ways of organising and communicating at their disposal, children may rely on narrative alone.

---

**Figure 2** Attainment Target 1: Reading
The development of the ability to read, understand and respond to all types of writing

---

**ATTAINMENT TARGET 1: READING**
Pupils should be able to

**LEVEL DESCRIPTION**

1 Recognise that print conveys meaning.
Show signs of developing an interest in books (e.g. by turning to them readily, looking at and talking about illustrations).
Respond positively to being read to (e.g. by listening attentively and by asking for more).
Show a developing sight vocabulary (i.e. of words recognised on sight).

2 Demonstrate an interest in stories and poems (e.g. by becoming engrossed when reading to themselves and by enjoying listening to stories and poems).
Say what has happened and what may happen in stories.
Show some understanding of the feelings and motives of characters.
Choose favourite stories and poems.
Express opinions on what they have read.
Read familiar stories and poems aloud with reasonable fluency and accuracy.
Display increasing independence, confidence, fluency, accuracy and understanding in reaching meaning in new reading material by using effectively more than one cueing strategy.
Demonstrate a sight vocabulary drawn from all areas of the curriculum and from out-of-school experiences.

3 Engage in sustained silent reading of stories.
Read aloud from familiar stories and poems fluently with appropriate expression.
Make confident and effective use of a variety of cueing strategies and reading experience to reach meaning.
Make some use of inference, deduction and reading experience to reach meanings which are beyond the literal.
Show developing understanding of the settings of stories, of how key events impinge on characters and of the reasons for their actions.
Continue to listen attentively to stories, showing an ability to recall details and a developing ability to discuss various aspects of stories.

4 Read regularly over a widening range of prose and verse.
Give reasons for establishing preferences.
Draw on reading experience to make comparisons and note parallels.
Show a developing familiarity with a number of basic kinds of narrative (children's fiction, legend, fable, folk tale, fantasy, science fiction, etc.).
Read aloud with increasing confidence and fluency from a range of familiar literature with appropriate expression.
Discuss aspects of a variety of books and poems in some detail, expressing opinions and providing supporting evidence from the text.

5 Read regularly and voluntarily over a still wider range of prose and verse.
Show developing tastes and preferences over an increased range of material.
Display fluency, adaptibility and accuracy when deploying a range of reading strategies, whether reading to themselves or aloud.
Show through discussion that they can use text to infer, deduce, predict, compare and evaluate.

## 3. The scope of English for ages 5–11

Current debate focuses upon assessment, recording, targets and achievements. The English Working Group made a useful initial contribution to that debate by their proposals illustrated in Figure 2.

However, there are other aspects of the report which had even more significance and long term value for the education of children with special educational needs. Four of these aspects will be highlighted here to show the far reaching nature of the recommendations: their focus on the learner; their balancing of extremes; their emphasis on entitlement to a full curriculum in English; their stress upon the integral nature of assessment activities.

### (a) The learner at the centre

After the crude attempts in *English from 5 to 16* (DES, 1984) to focus upon age-related objectives, the *Report of the Committee of Inquiry into the Teaching of English Language* – the Kingman Report (DES, 1988) – drew largely upon the discipline of linguistics to present a four-pronged model of English in terms of forms of language; communication and comprehension; acquisition and development; and historical and geographical variation. The report effectively made the case for teaching children *about* language but warned against a return to decontextualised exercises and 'old-fashioned formal teaching of grammar' (2.27) which describe Latin better than English. However, the report does not show from examples of good practice how the model can be sensitively applied, nor clearly show how its features are relevant to the study of English in schools. In this respect it remained disciplinary and external.

On the other hand, *English for ages 5–11* made a welcome return to child-centred learning, the needs of individuals and links between attainment targets and relevant practice. Its discussions of English in the primary school opened with a quotation from *Children and their Primary Schools* (CACE, 1967):

> At the heart of the educational process lies the child. No advances in policy, no acquisitions of new equipment have their desired effect unless they are in harmony with the nature of the child . . .

Members of the group recognised that the child with special educational needs would move less quickly through attainment levels and that within the different activities of English the child would probably be progressing at different rates (13.4). Level 1 may represent long term goals for those with severe learning difficulties but their achievements must be celebrated:

> When such children attain level 1, the fact that, despite their difficulties, they have started down the curricular path should be acknowledged as a real achievement. (13.5)

This positive view was carried through to suggestions for assessment activities – see (d) below.

### (b) Balancing of extremes

The working group discussed different views on the teaching of English under the following headings: personal growth, cross-curricular, adult needs, cultural heritage and cultural analysis. Whatever emphasis is placed by individuals, members insisted that English should enable:

> Children progressively to widen their language competence from the uses of home and family to those of the school, the work place and of society at large. (3.26)

For example, 'all children should have full access to Standard English', but without having their non-standard dialects denigrated, (4.24). In avoiding clear-cut recommendations for teaching Standard English the working group did not dodge the issue; rather it used insights into language as a system and applied them practically to the needs of individuals. So the understanding that 'dialect features are not errors' (4.18) underpin the statement that it is 'unrealistic to require children to speak Standard English in the classroom if it is not their native dialect, because many aspects of spoken production are automatic and below the level of conscious control' (4.14). This balancing of the needs of society and the needs of individual learners was helpful and reassuring.

Similarly the arguments for teaching children *about* language were clear and the actual examples given showed children learning about sentences and using linguistic terminology in real contexts. This is a more balanced view than appeared in some earlier reports. For example, the Kingman committee, on page 52, argue:

> It should be the entitlement of all pupils to be given the opportunity to attain the following targets:
>
> > Understand the syntax of phrases and sentences in Standard English, including that of complex sentences, and how the grammar of complex sentences related to complex temporal, spatial, causal and intentional relationships.

Even the reader who agrees with 'entitlement' will speculate how far most learners with special educational needs will develop the reflectiveness and explicitness to cope with such abstractions. Written like this, an attainment target directs teachers to teaching adverbial clauses of condition and concession together with the temptation to use decontextualised exercises as the means to that end. *English for Ages 5–11* is more practical in spelling out why the study of what language is and what it does can be fascinating and relevant for all children.

The Kingman Report asserted that learning about language 'increases possibilities of subtler expression' (p. 21) and enables 'children...to become effective members of a wide range of groups' (p. 10).

No evidence for either of these claims was offered. *English for Ages 5-11* trod on this ground more warily, but also without supporting evidence. Its tentativeness may be seen in the words italicised:

> *It is very plausible that* children's writing will be improved if they know more about language in general (5.18)

and

> performance *does, however, seem to be helped by* the systematic discussion of language in use (5.19).

For children with special educational needs there are more certain ways of developing ability to use language than by teaching about structure. But why this attempt to balance the issue? Perhaps because there were extreme views among politicians as well as among teachers. Another reason may well have been that it had been decided to fund a special project on language, beginning in 1989. LINC (Language in the National Curriculum) was generously funded by the department of Education and Science and local education authorities who provided more than twenty million pounds over a three year period 1989-92. The intention was to use expert trainers and a cascade method of in-service training to teach teachers about the model of language that the Kingman Committee (DES, 1988) had formulated.

## (c) *Entitlement to a full curriculum in English*

This is an issue that has already been mentioned, so it can be dealt with briefly. Importantly for pupils with special educational needs, the working group placed emphasis on the whole person: 'the personal and social development of the child are inextricably linked' (3.17) and on the organic unity of inter-active spoken language, reading and writing. The members had excellent things to say about areas integral to English, such as studying the media, information technology and drama, as well as about language study, writing, talk, reading and the central importance of literature. To all of these areas all learners should have access.

In the past 'disability' sometimes resulted in certain parts of the curriculum being perceived as 'inappropriate' or 'too difficult to modify'. Similarly, 'remediation' sometimes meant concentrating exclusively on those issues that were causing difficulty. These trends produced a shrunken curriculum and often intensified a sense of separateness, frustration and failure in learners who already had shaky self concepts. The working group said clearly that, where children's disabilities impaired 'their access to the curriculum this access should be facilitated by alternative means' (3.10).

Allowances also had to be made for access problems that initially hindered progress. They were forthright about practice which has hindered development rather than encouraging it. In reading, for example, they said:

> Teachers should recognise that reading is a complex but unitary process and not a set of discrete skills which can be taught separately in turn and, ultimately, bolted together. (9.7)

The child who is having difficulty with reading needs more than anyone to experience the pleasure and satisfaction that poems and stories can give. The same is true for children with specific disabilities such as impaired vision. Alternative access can be provided via 'large print books or optical or electronic devices for enlarging print, or...braille' (13.12). Such children also need to be read to frequently and to listen to books on tape.

### (d) The integral nature of assessment activities

The group recommended that assessment, whether by structured observation or the Standard Assessment Tasks (SATs) should be 'designed to resemble, and build on, normal classroom activities.' (7.17).

This continuity of assessment is important for all children, particularly for those with special educational needs. SATs should hold no terrors if they are truly 'designed to arise naturally out of good primary practice' and are 'coherent in structure and content'. The implication was that it would be helpful, for example, for those children having difficulty with reading to have no interruptions for testing by norm-referenced, outmoded tests which produce 'reading ages' of doubtful value and validity. The group recommended miscue analysis to record and evaluate children's errors and said that SATs' results;

> should be capable of being used formatively and to indicate any particular need for support for the child, or for more specific diagnostic assessment.

In this way assessment was perceived as organic and compatible with the notion of a continuum of ability.

The group also suggested that the appropriateness of assessment tasks be related to the severity of disabilities in the child. For example, children with various physical disabilities might have difficulty with writing and therefore might be exempted from the handwriting target. Braille, a word processor or dictation might be used instead. Similarly the speaking and listening component would need modifying for deaf children who might use signing, or speech along with signing. This kind of variation is compatible with an interactive notion of special educational needs and provision in schools.

52

## 4. Reservations

Inevitably with a report such as this there were reservations: some of these were to do with how the group's proposals might be changed detrimentally, as has already been mentioned; others were concerns as to how specific recommendations might be interpreted. For example, the group had been forced to work in two stages and it followed that its attainment levels 1–5 might be associated too rigidly with the primary school age range. Indeed this seemed to be the intention of the original terms of reference which referred to 'clear objectives for the knowledge, skills, understanding and aptitudes which pupils of different abilities and maturity should be expected to have acquired *at or near certain ages*' (my italics, 1.2). High achieving primary pupils of exceptional ability have special needs also and may require the provision of an assessment framework which also includes levels 6–10 and appropriate programmes of study. Some level descriptions were truncated and likely to be interpreted narrowly. For example, 'Show a developing sight vocabulary (i.e. of words recognised on sight)' in Level 1, **Attainment Target 1: Reading** (see Figure 2) failed to mention other strategies such as predicting meaning and guessing: which children are capable of at the outset of the reading journey.

However, the likely benefits of a sound, flexible, interactive programme to respond to the needs of a continuum of learners far outweighed the few negative features.

## 5. Running with a handicap

This analysis of the English working group's first report is a positive one. Despite certain reservations this chapter has concentrated upon the group's real achievements in balancing extremes, arguing for entitlement to a full curriculum in English, making organic the relationship between teaching and assessing and, above all, returning to a pupil-centred view of teaching and learning.

By early 1989 English was halfway there, but, as the introduction to this chapter has outlined, the frosty reception of the full report by its commissioners was the beginning of deliberate nobbling of the horse called English in the National Curriculum Handicap.

There are strong indications that a small central group of right wing politicians, who had originally handpicked membership of the English Working Group to produce a report in line with their own prescriptive predilections, began to feel in 1989 that somehow their English National Curriculum had been hi-jacked by liberal progressives. The National Curriculum Council's consultation procedures also seemed not to be capable of delivering what the Government required. Since that time handicaps of various kinds have been loaded on English in attempts to make it run securely under control and in the direction required. It is regrettable that ignorance and prejudice about language in learning and language in use provided the motivation for the distortions that ensued. In the context of certain outcomes of the Education Reform Act, the literacy and oracy futures for children with special educational needs now look far less rosy than they did a few years ago.

For example, it has become clear that some local education authorities are deliberately delaying statementing procedures, because of the financial implications of funding legislated provision. Older children with special educational needs are more frequently refused for employment training; since funding has been cut, preference may be given to those who can gain qualifications through examination success. The expense of providing specialised resources in mainstream schools for children with special educational needs sometimes persuades LEAs to keep those children in special schools when integrated learning may be best for the children's needs. At school level there is concern that children with special educational needs may tarnish a school's commercial and popular image. Open enrolment, Local Management of Schools and the requirement to have test results for schools published in league tables for easy comparison may combine to influence governors to exclude certain children, or at least ensure that they do not depress school scores.

These confusions are a result of political failure to see how some of the principles underlying the Education Acts of 1981 and 1988 are contradictory (Wade and Moore, 1992). More recent deliberate changes show political dogma at work, for example, in the way that the heads of NCC and SEAC have recently been replaced by government appointees. The LINC project, referred to earlier, is presently hampered by the decision of ministers not to publish its excellent training materials through HMSO. It seems it is dangerous to show how language is intimately related to cultures, values and to power relations. Further copies of *English for ages 5-11* and *English for ages 5-16* are not available and the flimsy originals disintegrate easily. The sturdy ringbinder *English in the National Curriculum* is built to last, but contains none of the crucial rationale of the original reports. Instead of the notion of a child-centred approach for those with special educational needs which works towards attainment targets, the teacher is now presented with targets at the front of the ringbinder. Certain shifts and excisions have been made from Attainment Targets as presented in *English for ages 5-16*. For example, level 10 of the Reading Attainment Target began:

(i). Read a range of poetry, fiction, literary non-fiction and drama, including works written before the 20th century and works from different cultures.

In the ringbinder version Angela Rumbold cut out the words 'from different cultures'. Although the programmes of study may support cultural diversity, as her letter to the *Times Educational Supplement* (15 June 1990) claimed, it is the Attainment Targets which are now foregrounded and some groups of children may now be disadvantaged. Mr. Clarke's decision to

54

reduce H.M. Inspectorate weakens a body which has provided information based on observation rather than dogma. H.M.I. have played an essential role in identifying and arguing for vulnerable groups of children, for example travellers' children who, largely as a result of H.M.I. efforts, now have access to schooling. It will in future be harder to identify and to provide for such educational needs.

Mr. Clarke piles on a further weight of handicap by his insistence that school results be presented to parents in their 'raw' state, whereas only a value-added approach can properly measure a school's performance. If, for example, certain lazy, suburban children with incompetent teachers continue to outperform other inner-city children with special educational needs and dedicated, imaginative teachers, what exactly does that mean? In the latter part of 1991 Mr. Clarke departed from the notion of Standard Assessment *Task*. The specifications for Key Stage 3 assessment require:

> timed, written *tests*, taken simultaneously by all pupils under controlled conditions.

It is as if diversity and special educational need did not exist. The plan is presently to test reading and writing separately from each other, despite the acknowledged interdependence of these modes in practice. Further, he intends to reduce the permissible percentage of English coursework from 100 per cent, in some cases, to about 30 per cent. This will have serious consequences for the least able students in secondary schools who have demonstrated increased motivation, less truancy and a higher standard of work in their English courses as a result of course work based assessment. A return to set texts, increased load upon memory and the pressure of examinations will not favour students with special educational needs.

English as a core subject is up and running, but its progress and promise for those with special educational needs could be made easier if some of the recent encumbrances were removed. We look to Mr Patten and future Secretaries of State for a positive lead.

### References

CACE, (1967) *Children and their Primary Schools*, (The Plowden Report). London: HMSO.
Cox, B. (1991) *Cox on Cox: an English Curriculum for the 1990's*. London: Hodder & Stoughton.
Department of Education and Science (1984) *English from 5 to 16*. London: HMSO.
Department of Education and Science (1988) *Report of the Committee of Inquiry into the Teaching of English Language*. (Kingman Report), London: HMSO.
DES & Welsh Office (1988) *English for ages 5 to 11*. HMSO.
DES & Welsh Office (1989) *English for ages 5-16*. HMSO.
DES & Welsh Office (1990) *English in the National Curriculum*. HMSO.
Payton, S. (1984) *Developing Awareness of Print*. Offset Publication No. 2, Educational Review Publications, Birmingham University.

Wade, B. (1984) *Story at Home and School.* Educational Review Occasional Publication No. 10, Birmingham University.

Wade, B. (1989) 'English: Half Way There', *British Journal of Special Education.* **16**, 1, pp. 6–9.

Wade, B. & Moore, M. (1992) *Patterns of Educational Integration: international perspectives on mainstreaming children with special educational needs.* Oxford: Triangle Books.

# CHAPTER 4

# History: Issues to Resolve

*Michael D. Wilson*

Following the National Curriculum History Working Group's interim and final reports, the DES published its final policy statement in March 1991: *History in the National Curriculum* (*England*) – hereafter abbreviated to HNC for ease of reference.

The purpose of this paper will be to:

I   provide an outline of the HNC document,
II  assess it critically, especially with regard to the teaching of history to pupils with special educational needs,
III conclude with some suggestions which may be regarded as crucial to successful implementation.

## I. The HNC Document: a general outline

There are several points which are to be commended.

(1) *Rationale*. First and foremost a clear rationale for the teaching of history in schools is stipulated (a total of two main aims and six other purposes) and, as such, articulates a formidable defence for its inclusion in the school curriculum.

(2) *Goals*. On the basis of the History Working Group's recommendations, the HNC document has set out to effect a number of major improvements. Especially important, for example, is the conscious attempt to establish both consistency and continuity between the primary and secondary phases of education. Moreover, in the light of the recent HMI report, *Aspects of Primary Education: The Teaching and Learning of History and Geography*, the need to 'fortify the position of history in primary schools' deserves to be

regarded as a major priority. All too frequently the foundations of meaningful history teaching are not laid until transfer to secondary school.

(3) *Course content.* The question of what history to include and what to omit, and of what balance to strike between skills and knowledge, will forever remain a bone of contention. However, the HNC document argues cogently in defence of the criteria behind the final selection. These are set out below:

(a) *Breadth and balance* are to be achieved through applying the so-called PESC formula to each history study unit (HSU), ensuring a political, economic, social and cultural perspective; through including a wide range of perspectives, both temporal (ancient to modern) and geographical (local to world); through including a wide range of skills which are central to the discipline of history (e.g. interpretation); and themes which cover long periods of time (concept of development) and shorter periods (depth).

(b) *Coherence* is to be achieved by ensuring that each HSU is capable of delivering the attainment targets (ATs), has links across each of the four key stages, and is taught within a chronological framework (regarded as fundamental to acquiring such key concepts as cause, consequence and continuity).

(c) *Establishing a rational balance* between local, British (not exclusively English), European and world history is the third criterion. Emphasis is clearly placed on local and British history on the grounds of relevance (the question of national heritage) and immediacy, but European and world themes are also included as valuable for their own sake – not just as a means of appreciating Britain's position in a wider context.

Proposals for compulsory content (core study units), at the four key stages, are summarised below. However, flexibility is also achieved through a wide range of supplementary study units, where selection is based on individual choice.

*Key Stage 1* has a single HSU introducing 'the past' and a 'sense of time', people (including family) within living memory, and historical personalities and events through stories.

*Key Stage 2* has five or six CSUs: invaders and settlers (Romans, Anglo-Saxons and Vikings in Britain); life in Tudor and Stuart times; Victorian Britain and/or Britain since 1930; Ancient Greece; and exploration and encounters 1450 to 1550. In addition, three or four supplementary units must be followed.

*Key Stage 3* includes five CSUs: the Roman Empire; Medieval realms 1066–1500; the making of the U.K. 1500–1750; expansion, trade and industry in Britain 1750–1900; and the era of the Second World War. There are also three supplementary units.

*Key Stage 4* prescribes one CSU; Britain, Europe and the world in the twentieth century.

(4) *Assessment and reporting.* The purpose is clearly specified: to ensure that individual pupils are making progress; to keep parents and other teachers informed of such progress; and to build up a record of evidence of each pupil's attainments, with implications for the next key stage of learning. The document therefore specifies:

(a) Three attainment targets (ATs):

    (i) Knowledge and Understanding of History (including change/time, cause/consequence, similarity/difference, empathy).

    (ii) Interpretations of history.

    (iii) Use of sources.

(b) The amplifying of each AT into statements of attainment (SOAs) at 10 levels, covering the four key stages.

(c) Programmes of study (PoS) specified as means of achieving the ATs.

It is worth pointing out that the History Working Group had resisted pressure to propose a separate AT for historical knowledge. In response to the problems highlighted, the final policy statement ascribes knowledge (exclusively of factual content) to the PoS, not the ATs. In respect of attainment, knowledge means both knowledge of specific historical content and knowledge in a broader sense, e.g. 'knowing . . . that historical events usually have more than one cause and consequence'. In other words, it has been recognised that the concept of 'knowledge' is meaningless without understanding and its integration within all the stated ATs.

(5) *Implementation and Planning.* Detailed guidelines for schools and history departments are provided in a wide range of key issues, such as curriculum and development plans, study units and schemes of work at each key stage (e.g. criteria for selection, the sequencing of units), time allocation, coping with mixed classes of pupils at different stages, cross-curricular links (with other subjects and with regard to common skills, including IT). A useful framework is also provided for appropriate teaching methods (including the use of source material and catering for individual needs) and the promotion of equal opportunities.

## II. Assessing the HNC document with regard to special educational needs

There are principles highlighted in the policy statement which history teachers of pupils with special educational needs should welcome.

(1) The implication that history is of value to all children is apparent, although this is more directly stated in the final report of the History Working Group, which emphasised the importance of 'access' and 'curriculum entitlement'. In a section on special educational needs (Final Report, 1990, p. 171) it stated:

> 'History is accessible and of value to all pupils although assessment techniques and arrangements have not always been appropriate to pupils with special educational needs.
>
> It is important that due regard is taken of the difficulties faced by individual pupils, especially in ensuring that they are not, inadvertently, excluded from showing what they can achieve by the nature of the tasks set for assessment purposes.'

(2) The scope of 'special educational needs' is seen as including not only those children with physical, sensory and speech difficulties but also exceptionally able pupils who 'should be challenged rather than simply expected to produce more written work'. This can be accomplished by providing opportunities for discussion and further research, so that these children can tackle more complex issues, understand more difficult concepts, deepen and broaden their know-ledge/understanding, and use a wider/more demanding range of sources. (section C20, paras 11.10, 11.11).

(3) Useful and highly specific advice is provided for teachers in facilitating 'access' for children with learning difficulties, including:

(i) Making complex historical content easier for pupils to understand (e.g. through concrete examples, practical activities, flexibility regarding rates and levels of study).

(ii) Breaking tasks down into small sequential steps.

(iii) Selecting material which interests/motivates children with behavioural difficulties.

(iv) Providing a rich variety of source materials (e.g. artefacts and reading material carefully selected for layout, language level and content) and activities (e.g. the use of drama, videos and IT).

(v) Helping children with specific handicaps (e.g. through the use of tape recorders, non-sighted methods of reading, such as Braille, and various technological aids, including word-processors, to assist in producing written work).

(vi) Flexible interpretation of the requirements of the PoS, wherever possible adapting activities to the needs of individual pupils. In a minority of cases this will require modifications to schemes of work wholly or partly based on an earlier key stage, or disappli-cation of the History Order for 'the very small minority of pupils for whom a greater degree of flexibility is required'. (Section C19/20, para. 11.1 to 11.9; NCC, *Curriculum Guidance 2.*).

(4)    Some of the more general policy statements should provide a framework for good practice. These may be identified below:

(i)    The weighting of HSUs in favour of British and local history. Arguably, this approach will root history in the child's immediate experience and proceed from the familiar to the unfamiliar (e.g. HSU 1, Level 1, links the study of history initially to the family and immediate contacts). The value of local history, both in its immediacy and the opportunities it affords for practical investigation, has been emphasised by others with reference to special educational needs (e.g. Wilson, 1985, pp. 46–47; McIver, 1982, pp. 125–126).

(ii)   Attainment targets are clearly defined, each with 10 levels of attainment. In principle, these Orders are consistent with an assessment procedure linked to carefully planned progressions and establishing mastery at each stage (through reinforcement and remediation, as appropriate) before moving on to higher levels. So-called 'mastery learning' has long found favour with teachers of pupils with special educational needs.

The first five levels of attainment, which should cater for the great majority of children with learning difficulties (aged 5 to 16) are summarised in Figure 1. For the gifted child, it is stipulated that the overall progression through the key stages should not be disturbed, rather that such pupils should have their skills and understanding enriched within the key stages.

(iii)  Guidelines on teaching methods and the use of resources are clearly aimed at bringing history to life. Reference is made to such approaches as using field trips; museum and site visits; drama and role play; the use of rich, varied literary resources; radio, TV, film, oral history and archaeology. Bringing history to life is essential in motivating all children, but particularly those with learning difficulties.

Finally it should be emphasised that several problems arising from the History Working Group's final report have been addressed in the HNC document, notably:

(i)    The prescriptive nature of the report – far more flexibility has been built into the final policy statement regarding such matters as the selection of subject content (cf. the supplementary study units); modifications permitted in the interests of individual needs; and the application of the PESC formula, which is now envisaged as a framework for ensuring balance rather than a strait-jacket for each and every HSU.

**Figure 1** History Statements of Attainment: A Summary of Levels 1 to 5

| | AT1 (a) Change + Time AT1 = 'Knowledge and understanding of History' | AT1 (b) Cause + Consequence | AT1 (c) Similarity + Difference | AT1 (c) Empathy | AT2 Interpretations of History | AT3 Use of Sources |
|---|---|---|---|---|---|---|
| Level 1 | Place in sequence events in a story about the past. | Give reasons for their own actions. | | Not applicable. | Understand that stories may be about real people or fictional characters. | Communicate information from a historical source. |
| Level 2 | Place familiar objects in chronological order. | Suggest reasons why people in the past acted as they did. | Identify differences between past and present times. | | Show an awareness that different stories about the past can give different versions of what happened. | Recognise that historical sources can stimulate and help answer questions about the past. |
| Level 3 | Describe changes over a period of time. | Give reasons for an historical event/development. | Identify differences between times in the past. | | Distinguish between fact and point of view. | Make deductions from historical sources. |
| Level 4 | Recognise that over time some things change, others stay the same. | Historical events usually have more than one cause and consequence. | Describe different features of an historical situation. | | Show an understanding that deficiencies in evidence may lead to different interpretations of the past. | Put together information from different historical sources. |
| Level 5 | Distinguish between types of historical change (rapid/gra-dual/local/national). | Identify different types of cause and consequence (long/short term). | Describe different features of an historical period. | | Recognise that accounts of the past may differ from what is known to have happened. | Comment on the usefulness of an historical source, by reference to its content, as evidence for a particular enquiry. |

(ii)   The whole approach to assessment and differentiation – the recommendations from the advisers in history, that the number of ATs should be reduced from four to three, have been implemented with the welcome prospect that teachers will be able to spend a greater proportion of their time actually teaching rather than needlessly assessing and recording (notwithstanding the importance of assessment and recording in the right measure). On the question of differentiation (on the basis of ability) the History Working Group report clearly recommended differentiation on the basis of *outcome* (Final Report p. 168). Differentiation by *input* (in terms of planned teaching strategies, selection of resources and planned pupil activities) was hardly addressed. This is no longer the case, as the History Orders provide substantial guidelines on teaching and learning strategies to meet individual needs (as outlined above).

(iii)  The final report of the History Working Group introduced abstract ideas that appeared inappropriate to children's conceptual development (e.g. the Civil War unit at Key Stage 2 required an understanding of such concepts as 'aristocracy', 'gentry' and 'yeomanry', which many eight-to-nine-year olds – let alone pupils with learning difficulties – would have difficulty in grasping. Significantly, in the final policy statement, we now read of amended concepts like 'rulers' and 'people in town and county'. Clearly, this has been a problem which the HNC policy statement has directly addressed.

Having reviewed the HNC document, especially with regard to special/individual needs, it can be said that there is much that is positively helpful and encouraging. However, attention needs to be drawn to a number of crucial issues if the successful implementation of the History National Curriculum is to be assured.

### III. Suggestions crucial to successful implementation

If the policy statement is to work effectively in schools then a number of problems should be anticipated and, as far as possible, prevented. The following are especially important.

(i)    There will have to be adequate resources. The History Working Group's final report itself acknowledged this fact with regard to curriculum resources (e.g. textbooks) and teacher training. I would go further. There will also be a demand for increased resources to create an appropriate management structure in schools to ensure that the national history curriculum is carried out successfully. Additional responsibility allowances should be found for such posts as:

*Co-ordinators* for specific subject areas (including history) at the primary stage to provide team leadership and manage specialist resources (bearing in mind the lack of subject specialists in primary schools as well as in some special schools, in many subject areas).

*Key teachers* (on the lines advocated by Thomas and Jackson, 1986) in specific subject areas in secondary schools, to co-ordinate the work of the department in meeting special educational needs and liaising with the learning support/special needs department in ensuring that the skills of support teachers are infused across the curriculum.

(ii)   Schools will require far more detailed and specific guidelines on assessment and recording strategies with regard to teaching history to pupils with learning difficulties. This is acknowledged by the HNC policy statement (section E), which makes reference to the fact that 'further guidance on assessment, recording and reporting will be issued by the Schools Examinations and Assessment Council'. What is particularly disturbing, to quote Ian Nash, is that 'Some of the most successful courses ever devised for raising the achievement of low attaining pupils will be abolished under Government plans to restrict assessed coursework in GCSE to 20 per cent'. (TES, 8 Nov. 1991). Although this reference is not directly concerned with the teaching of history, it raises the wider issue of identifying the assessment procedures that will most effectively demonstrate what pupils with learning difficulties can actually achieve. This, I suspect, will not be accomplished by insisting on a narrow definition of attainment in terms of expertise in a written examination; rather it is likely to be achieved through employing a wide range of carefully selected assessment procedures, adumbrated in the HNC document itself.

(iii)  Programmes of research will be needed to monitor and evaluate the implementation of the History National Curriculum in schools, with a focus on children with special needs (both the exceptionally able and those with learning difficulties). This is where H.M.I. could render an invaluable service, but its future role is currently in doubt. Whatever the case, longitudinal studies which measure performance and standards over a period of time against set criteria will be essential. Similarly, more research needs to be done on the way children acquire historical understanding, before an appropriate number of attainment levels can be established with any reasonable degree of objectivity. For the time being, the stipulated 10 levels provide a framework and a focus for targeting teaching and learning objectives, but future modification (if not simplification) may well result from a greater understanding of the psychology of the learning of history.

In conclusion, I would argue that the question of funding is paramount. The Government must show commitment to its far-reaching educational

64

reforms by ensuring that they are adequately funded. But it must also be said that in an age of LMS the allocation of those valuable resources will depend on the perceived priorities of school management, regarding such crucial matters as the allocation of curricular time for history, the allocation of teaching/learning resources, and the provision of in-service training. If the ideals of 'equal opportunities', 'access' and 'entitlement' for all are to be more than just cosmetic embellishments to enlightened curricular aims and objectives, then the question of special needs will figure highly in every school's list of priorities.

## References

Department of Education and Science (1989) *Aspects of Primary Education: The Teaching and Learning of History and Geography*. (HMI Report). London: HMSO.

Department of Education and Science (1989) *National Curriculum History Working Group: Interim Report*. London: HMSO.

Department of Education and Science (1990) *National Curriculum History Working Group: Final Report*. London: HMSO.

Department of Education and Science (1991) *History in the National Curriculum (England)*. London: HMSO.

McIver, V. (ed.) (1982) *Teaching History to Slow Learning Children in Secondary Schools*. Belfast: Queen's University.

Thomas, G. and Jackson, B. (1986) The Whole School Approach to Integration. *British Journal of Special Education*. **13**, 1, 27–39.

*Times Educational Supplement*, 8 November 1991.

Wilson, M. D. (1985) *History for Pupils with Learning Difficulties*. London: Hodder & Stoughton.

Wilson, M. D. (1990) History: Issues to Resolve, *British Journal of Special Education*, **17**, 2, 69–71.

# CHAPTER 5

# Geography: Another Time, Another Place

*John Clarke*

Teachers began to implement National Curriculum Geography in September 1991 in Key Stages 1, 2 and 3. There are a number of challenges in this process.

In the first place many teachers, particularly in primary schools, have not taught this sort of Geography before – and even where they have, frequently need persuading that they have.

In the second place, there is a tension between the way in which Geography, traditionally, has been taught, again particularly in primary schools, and the demands of National Curriculum Geography. Traditionally, Geography has been integrated with other subjects, notably History, and while this is still possible in the National Curriculum era, integration places further burdens upon teachers in terms of classroom planning and in terms of assessment practices which fit the constraints of National Curriculum Assessment.

Thirdly, there is a very big resource issue. Simply, schools do not have all the resources necessary to teach National Curriculum in Geography. Where resources do exist they are frequently appropriate to the wrong levels in terms of attainment targets. More frequently they simply do not exist in the numbers required.

Further, National Curriculum Geography has been introduced at the same time as History but after Technology and the core subjects. Assessment issues in these latter are taking considerable time and are deflecting teachers' attention from introducing the new subjects – again, specifically in primary schools.

The conclusion is that the introduction of Geography is not happening in isolation but at a time when so many other developments are taking place. It is not easy for any teacher to introduce it, especially those in primary schools.

If it is not fully embedded into the curriculum at this stage it is not very surprising and if teachers are failing to meet the individual needs of all pupils in Geography at this time, that too is not surprising. In fact, it would be a miracle if they were.

Nevertheless, there are considerable faults in the design and presentation of National Curriculum Geography which make it very unlikely that the needs of all children, even in mainstream, will ever be met within it. Exceptional teachers are required to meet these needs in Geography, and schools, by definition, are not full of exceptional teachers. More cogent thinking by the Geography Working Group, the National Curriculum Council and the Department of Education and Science in designing the Statutory Order for Geography – and they, collectively, certainly had enough advice on this – might have made it possible for most teachers to teach the subject taking account of the different needs and previous attainments of their pupils. As it stands, in most classrooms this will not happen. It is unlikely that access to the geography curriculum and the exciting learning experiences which geography should generate can be an entitlement for all.

This chapter identifies the reasons for this through an analysis of the statutory order for Geography.

The Order sets five attainment targets (AT), three concerned with themes in geography – physical, human and environmental; one AT is concerned with geographical skills and one is concerned with locational knowledge and understanding. Although many geographers and geography teachers would argue that there should be an attainment target which more precisely addresses the geographical enquiry process, in fact, there is little to quarrel with in attainment targets on themes and skills.

The real problem lies with AT2 'Knowledge and Understanding of Places'. Although the degree of content prescription is less than was proposed in the interim report of the Geography Working Group and this is applauded by teachers, there remains a rump of prescribed content and precise pieces of place knowledge are required. Among a host of other things, by cross referencing to maps in the Programmes of Study, pupils at level 3 would be required to identify and name:

> The seven continents, the oceans, Caribbean Sea, North Pole, South Pole, Equator, Tropic of Cancer, and Tropic of Capricorn.
>
> Canada, USA, USSR, India, China, Japan, Australia, New York, Moscow, Tokyo.
>
> Rocky Mountains, Andes, Sahara Desert, Himalayas.
>
> River Mississippi, Amazon, Nile.
>
> Panama and Suez Canal.

For level 5 they would need to identify and name:

*the Arctic Circle, Antarctic Circle, Prime Meridian and International Date Line;*

*Mexico, Peru, Brazil, Venezuela, Argentina, Nigeria, China, South Africa, Kenya, Egypt, Israel, Saudi Arabia, Pakistan, Bangladesh, Indonesia, New Zealand;*

*Toronto, Washington DC, Chicago, San Francisco, Los Angeles, Mexico City, Lima, Sao Paulo, Buenos Aires, Caracas, Accra, Johannesburg, Lagos, Cairo, Jerusalem, Leningrad, Delhi, Bombay, Calcutta, Singapore, Jakarta, Beijing, Shanghai, Sydney;*

*the Rivers St. Lawrence, Great Lakes, Colorado, Congo (Zaire), Zambezi, Volga, Ganges, Yangtze, Murray-Darling.*

and on maps of the British Isles and Europe (Fig. 1):

*Glasgow, Newcastle, Leeds, Manchester, Liverpool, Birmingham, Bristol, Southampton, Paris, Berlin, Rome, Amsterdam, Copenhagen, Brussels, Madrid, Lisbon, Athens;*

*France, Germany, Italy, Denmark, Netherlands, Luxembourg, Belgium, Spain, Portugal, Greece;*

*the Mediterranean Sea and the Rivers Rhine and Danube.*

This list of content is merely intended to be a baseline. There is an expectation in the report that teachers will extend the context of study to include other places in Europe and the world. Nevertheless, there is a danger that this baseline will define the world for pupils in schools – an interesting prospect in itself when the world, in respect of the USSR has already changed. The proposed curriculum is extensive and requires, according to the Working Group, a minimum equivalent of three periods out of a 40-period week, for five-to-13-year-olds, to cover it adequately. This is more than is currently available in most secondary schools and, according to HMI surveys, considerably more than is currently available in primary schools where many will be beginning National Curriculum Geography from a long way behind the starting line (HMI, 1989). This is also likely to be the situation in many special schools.

However, there is a more disturbing aspect to this prescription of content in this attainment target. The tradition, certainly in secondary schools, is of children being taught as groups or whole classes. The individualised curriculum is a very long way off and there are good reasons why this should be so. Much curriculum development work in geography over the last ten years has centred on teaching and learning strategies where lessons, both in and outside the classroom, are made more active and collaborative. This, in turn, has made the geography classroom a more exciting place and a place where children who do not find geography easy are likely to achieve more than in the traditional classroom.

The desire for children to be more than passive recipients of the curriculum in geography has involved such techniques as role play, simulations, jigsawing – structuring activities to ensure that every pupil takes part (Johnson and Johnson, 1984) – decision making and problem solving in groups, as well as fieldwork inquiries. The developments have been towards making pupils part of a group experience where what each child does is important because it affects the learning of the whole group. Such an activity might, for example, involve splitting a location into areas where different groups of pupils collect different data as part of a whole class project. Equally, children might be encouraged to work in small groups to identify the particular interests of those concerned with the management of the Amazonian rain forest and then to take part in role play to defend those interests. These are whole class activities designed to involve children in their own learning and to place a responsibility on each pupil for the quality of the learning of the whole group. In terms of the meeting of individual needs these teaching strategies have been designed to ensure a greater level of involvement from all pupils, especially those for whom geography, for one reason or another, is not easy.

It is these developments which are under threat from the geography proposals. There is likely to be a major problem for teachers working with pupils in Key Stages 2 to 4. It is much less of a problem for those working in Key Stage 1 and should present few difficulties for those teachers in special schools who are working with pupils within levels 1 to 3. At these levels, and perhaps beyond, the programmes of study and attainment targets should not cause serious difficulties for most special schools, apart from teachers' probable unfamiliarity with the geographical subject matter, and the consequent need for them to acquire the knowledge and use imagunation in teaching it.

Some help for teachers in special schools is given in the Non Statutory Guidance for Geography (NCC, 1991, p. 26) and there is an excellent example of how to make the subject accessible to pupils with severe learning difficulties. Further, there are encouraging statements which relate to pupils with physical or sensory disabilities.

However the problems really begin in mainstream schools, at the upper end of primary and throughout the secondary years. It is easy and depressing to imagine the possible scene in year 8 classes, for example, by the end of the 1990s. The effects will be disguised in the short term because of the phasing arrangements. In September 1991 teachers in Key Stage 3 will begin with level 3, that being the start of the key stage which is intended to cater for levels 3 to 7. All children will be started on work from the programme of study which leads toward success at level 3 in the seven attainment targets. By 1995, however, children will come from primary schools having already completed Key Stage 2 and will display a range of previous attainments.

They will arrive at their secondary schools with profiles which may well resemble an urban skyline – soaring skywards in some attainment targets but not far off the ground in others. For each pupil the profile will be unique; some profiles will resemble the Manhattan skyline, others Copenhagen and others, Rochdale. The teacher's task will be to build on that profile and to offer a range of curricular experiences which is appropriate to each individual. The time for starting everyone at level 3 will be gone. To do so would be to risk parental wrath and the legitimate complaint that some sons and daughters had already achieved that level in their primary years. Certainly, through the system of reporting, parents will know what levels of attainment their children had achieved.

Teachers will have to develop strategies to cope with the challenge of having children in their classes with a range of previous achievements that stretch from Level 5 at its highest to level 2, and even below. Setting pupils into more homogeneous groupings may make the task easier but even then each pupil will have achieved differently on all attainment targets and therefore demonstrate different strengths and weaknesses, even in the same National Curriculum subject. Teachers will have to cope with the diversity they face. It will be very difficult to employ the recently vaunted 'whole class' teaching methods and differentiate the curriculum at the same time.

In some subject areas there are no problems beyond those currently faced by teachers who daily have to teach classes which are, by definition, composed of pupils with different attainments. In English, design and information technology capability, and in history, problems of defferentiation are no greater in the National Curriculum than they were before the National Curriculum.

The crucial point is that the attainment targets in these subjects are process based; they are not dependent upon specific content. For example, while pupils would have to demonstrate attainment in acquiring and evaluating evidence in history, there are no lists of the precise evidence they must acquire and evaluate. As they become more sophisticated in their evidence-handling skills they will use more sophisticated techniques in examining the evidence available for whatever historical topic the class as a whole is covering at the time. Difficult though it may be to achieve, all the teacher has to do is to ensure that there is a sufficient variety of course material in the classroom and a range of teaching styles to allow a range of children at different levels within that attainment target to achieve.

This is not so in geography. The existence of an attainment target which is based on prescribed content makes differentiation extremely difficult to achieve in the group situation. The National Curriculum is intended to be a curriculum based on progression. Once one level has been mastered the individual pupil moves on to work which eventually will lead to success at the next level. The implication is clear. In terms of Attainment Targets teachers would have to organise their classes into several groups all looking at different content. For example, some pupils would need to be

70

working on mastering the 'sources of power used in the USA or the USSR or Japan and explain the extent to which these have influenced the location and development of manufacturing industry in that country' (Level 6, statement e, AT4) while others, at the same time and in the same class, would need to be working on material which enabled them to 'examine and give an account of an important issue that has arisen from changes or proposed changes in a tropical or sub-tropical locality' (Level 4, statement d, AT4). Through careful collection and creation of resources this is not an impossible task for teachers to achieve but it is likely to lead to ineffective classroom practice.

Mortimore's study of junior school practice in the Inner London Education Authority (Mortimore *et al.*, 1988) identified that, where more than three activities from different curricular areas were taking place in the same classroom at the same time, pupil performance over a range of measures tended to be adversely affected. Opportunities for communication between teachers and pupils were reduced, pupil industry was lower, noise and pupil movement were greater. It seems that in mixed activity sessions the demands on teachers' time, attention and energy can become too great to ensure effective learning.

If this is true for junior schools it is far more likely to be true in secondary schools where there is little tradition of working in this way. It is, however, precisely this kind of classroom organisation which teachers in mainstream schools will be forced to adopt if the geography proposals are accepted. From the middle of Key Stage 2 until the end of Key Stage 4 it simply will not be possible for the whole class to be engaged on studying the same places at the same time and ensure that the needs of all the pupils are met. Moreover, opportunities for collaborative learning are severely diminished. The exciting approaches to the teaching of geography developed over the last few years will be abandoned in favour of a much more sterile approach. In this scenario, the strong likelihood is that children with special needs will be disadvantaged most. Strategies for whole class involvement with differentiated material will not work where pupils have to address different content. Children are more likely to work from printed task sheets provided by teachers to suit the different levels. The teacher, as in the worst practice in some maths classes, is in danger of becoming a deskilled ticker as pupils follow their lonely journey through their worksheets.

### References

Department of Education and Science (1990) *Geography for Ages 5-16*. London: DES.
Department of Education and Science (1989) *Aspects of Primary Education: The Teaching and Learning of History and Geography*. (HMI Report) London: HMSO.

Johnson, D. W. and Johnson, R. T. (1984) *Circles of Learning: Cooperation in the Classroom*. Washington DC: Association for Supervision and Curriculum Development.

Mortimore, P., Sammons, P., Stoll, L., Lewis, D. and Ecob, R. (1988) *School Matters*. Wells: Open Books.

CHAPTER 6

# The Introduction of a Modern Foreign Language into the Special School Curriculum

*Ruth Nichols* and *Gwen Thomas*

A pilot project, introducing French to groups of children with both moderate and severe learning difficulties, was initiated in the autumn of 1989 in seven Berkshire special schools. This paper follows the development of the programme up to the date of publication of the orders (*1*). In spite of initial doubts in the schools as to whether the addition of a modern language to the special school curriculum was desirable, or would be successful, all the schools which had access to an interested teacher with competence in French agreed to take part. The final report of the Working Group commended the principle that all pupils should have the opportunity to experience a modern foreign language (*2:13.3*), but that those directly involved in the education of the individual child should have the discretion to modify or disapply this area (*2:13.5*); in fact very few pupils were excluded, apart from children with profound and multiple handicaps and those with no oral communication.

The introduction of a modern foreign language into the school curriculum at Year 7 represents a new learning experience for most children, one in which children in the special school will, like their peers in mainstream schools, be working at Level 1. It also means that previous patterns of success or failure in learning may be no longer as relevant. For example, children from ethnic minority groups whose first language is not English and who, for this reason, may have appeared to be performing less well in the curriculum, may be able to demonstrate their language skills as they are often already sensitized to language differences.

(*1*) *Modern Languages in the National Curriculum, November 1991.*
(*2*) *Final Report of the Working Group on Modern Foreign Languages for ages 11 to 16, 1990.*

A modern language classroom in a special school already has teachers trained and practised in the methodology of first language development. In the evaluation reports consideration is given to the extent to which this methodology is transferable to second language learning and the ways in which this helps the teacher identify general and individual problems in language acquisition. Teachers in special schools work with small groups, and are thus able to differentiate tasks and goals; they often teach across a range of subjects, which gives them the opportunity to reinforce learning in a variety of contexts. Many children arrive in special schools with a sense of failure and the teachers are skilled in identifying activities and goals which motivate the individual child and which foster success. The teachers use finely graded objectives to restore to the child a sense of progression and achievement. They are sensitive to the need to generalize skills which may become set within the context in which they are taught. Teaching materials are selected to give the child multi-sensory experience and to avoid ambiguity: teachers use real objects before models, images or other forms of representation. Movement, role play, songs, action rhymes and drama are all used to develop the child's confidence and communication skills.

**Evaluation of the pilot programme**

The project has been externally evaluated twice, first in the Spring term, 1990; and then in the Autumn term, 1991. In the late spring of 1990, the present writers visited the schools, observed lessons and talked to the teachers. One of the teachers' monthly meetings was joined by an evaluator.

*First evaluation, Spring 1990*

As the initial advice of the Working Group was not available when the visits were planned, three general criteria were identified as appropriate in evaluating the pilot scheme. These were that the scheme should:

- provide the children with a new learning experience without adding to a previous history of failure;
- extend the children's linguistic experience;
- give the children an awareness of other people, places and cultures.

These general criteria were initially regarded as being more appropriate in the context of the evaluation than any more specific assessment of attainment in separate language skills. It was clear, however, that the children's progress, even after a few months or even weeks of the programme, was measurable. As the proposals of the Working Group were then published it was possible to match the observations with the general criteria outlined in the working group's proposals (*2:Ch.3*) and also with the attainment targets set out in the document (*2:Ch.5*). A summary follows of

74

lesson content and activities in the four attainment targets, observed at that time. (The revised wording from the final orders is used.)

---

**Attainment Target 1\*: Listening**
The development of the pupils' ability to understand and to respond to spoken language.

---

Lesson content
Physical response to classroom instructions.
Selecting and matching appropriate objects and flashcards.
Miming in response to the teacher's instructions.

Activities
Preparing and serving drinks and croissants in the Home Economics room.
Counting, sorting, and matching into sets in a practical mathematics lesson.
Exercises in aural discrimination, the identification of known phrases in unknown French.

Achievement
Many children had achieved the Level 1 statements of attainment for receptive language, responding to individual words and simple phrases in context.

---

**Attainment Target 2: Speaking**
The development of the pupils' ability to communicate in speech.

---

Lesson content
Greeting, talking about oneself, weather, colours and numbers.
Selecting and naming objects and flashcards.
Simple shopping and cafe situations using money.

Activities
Linked role play as in a street scene.
Exchanges between children as well as direct responses to the teacher.
The use of the normal registration period.
Greeting visitors.
A miming game where the group guessed the weather depicted.

Achievement
It was noticeable that in this area children of different abilities were soon performing differently: where one child would offer a single word comment, others would volunteer 3–4 phrases, e.g. *"C'est un/une..."*, *"J'ai* (number and noun)*..."*; *"J'aime...* or even *"Je n'aime pas..."*.

> **Attainment Target 3: Reading**
> The development of the pupils' ability to read, understand and respond to written language.

## Materials
Dual language labels around the class and the school, *Le coin français*, French posters and authentic materials.
French picture dictionaries, illustrated children's books, labels and flash cards.

## Activities
Most teachers had not embarked on formal teaching of the printed word. Some groups had adopted French names and could recognize labels and flashcards supported by images. Children were beginning to play word recognition games.

## Achievement
Pupils were beginning to match labels and to substitute words in sentences but, as in their English, reading was lagging behind aural skills.

> **Attainment Target 4: Writing**
> The development of the pupils' ability to communicate in writing.

## Lesson content
Labelling, copying, gap-filling exercises.

## Activities
Setting up labelled displays
Form filling with personal details
Project folders with material in both French and English.

## Achievements
It was interesting to find that, at the level of literacy appropriate to the pupils' development of English reading and writing, they found no greater difficulty in recording and responding in French.

In the first report on the project (*3*) the following observations were made:

*Length of lesson and size of group*: frequent and short (20–25 minute) lessons, with a group of 8–10 children, seemed to offer the best situation for intensive oral work, although a skilled teacher was observed giving an hour-long lesson with a wide variety of activities.

(*3*)'Foreign languages for all', *BJSE*, Vol. 18, No. 1, 1991. 'Pas comme les autres?' *Language Teaching Journal*, No. 4, 1991.

*Children's attitudes and achievements*: The children were responding with enthusiasm and with a high level of sustained concentration. The children were learning and retaining and their oral skills were developing. The children in most of the schools expressed their pride in tackling a subject that they knew had been confined to mainstream provision.

*Language proficiency*: Most teachers were over-anxious about their own language limitations.

*Methodology and materials*: There was limited awareness of foreign language methodology and the use of supplementary materials and activities, and of the way that these can contribute to the teachers' self-confidence and can enable them to exploit fully their knowledge of the language as well as adding interest and variety to the lessons.

The best lessons included: the sustained use of the target language by the teacher; a range of short (5–10 minute) language activities, some requiring verbal responses, some non-verbal; the use of audio-visual aids or objects that the children could handle; movement and gesture; situations where children had to modify their responses, rather than merely modelling; and situations where children could initiate exchanges.

The evaluation report concluded that there was no evidence that children with special needs should lose their entitlement to learning a foreign language; the conditions of a special school (small teaching groups and the expertise of the teachers) provided a secure learning environment. In some cases, the environment was over-protective and insufficient demands were made on the children. Questions were raised as to how far, and how long a foreign language programme could be sustained, when progressively greater demands would be made on the children's ability. Teacher supply and expertise might become problematic with the extension of the programme. Few of the project teachers wished to extend the time they gave to foreign language teaching. It was suggested that consideration could be given to the wider benefits to the children of the foreign language programme. Further inservice training, the extension of contacts with more experienced language teachers and the need for additional resources were recommended to the Authority.

## Evaluation, Autumn 1991

In this second report some proposals were given for criteria for modern foreign language teaching in special schools to children with learning difficulties. Two contrasting examples of good practice were given to highlight the importance of methodological expertise.

*Criteria for language teaching in the special school:*

- the sustained use of the target language as the medium for communication during the lesson as well as for the taught content;
- visual support for language;
- the encouragement of the 'ludic' aspects of language (the use of play);
- the differentiation of tasks set;
- the active physical involvement of the pupils;
- an element of *'civilisation'*.

## Contrasting examples of good practice

### Example one

A class of 13 children, aged 14+, with moderate learning difficulties, lesson lasting just under an hour. (These children had had one term of French a year earlier, followed by a break of a year; they will now continue French for two years, with one hour-long lesson a week).

### Lesson structure

(a)  rapid revision of greetings;
(b)  revision of vocabulary with picture flashcards;
(c)  introduction of word cards, intensive practice of matching word and picture;
(d)  word recognition without picture;
(e)  memory game with word flashcards only;
(f)  sound/meaning discrimination exercises: children identifying known phrases and questions embedded in unknown language;
(g)  revision of words with reading flashcards (some use of English to explain activities);
(h)  a song 'for Europe', composed by the teacher and sung as a round, accompanied by the teacher on a keyboard;
(i)  individual tasks: (instructions given in English) using concept keyboard, language master, word search from letter grids, setting up a display of matched pictures and words, labelling other displays. The teacher kept a running record of the tasks undertaken by the pupils.

### Example two

A class of 10 children, aged 9–10, with moderate and severe learning difficulties, lesson lasting 20 minutes. (These children had been learning French for two years.) Many children were spontaneously using French before the lesson started formally.

*Lesson structure*

(a)  revision of greetings, already initiated by the children;
(b)  revision of colours, using classroom objects and children's clothes;
(c)  introduction of new colours, using the same linguistic structures
      and the same material.

The children were actively involved and often volunteered comments, using the required structures or others learned earlier. A very high proportion of the time was taken up by the children's contributions.

These were two very different lessons, both given by teachers competent in the language, and both demonstrating a high degree of understanding of method. The first was highly organized, making expert use of a range of very attractive visual material and of supplementary, individualized teaching aids, from worksheet to computer. The children's learning was being carefully controlled, and most activities had very clear general, as well as specific, educational aims, e.g. individual responsibility, memory training, aural discrimination, the encouragement of body language and facial expression. The second had fewer and much simpler visual aids and relied much more on classroom objects and the children themselves. The lesson was not overtly 'organized' in a sequence of different activities, though the structuring of reinforcement and the introduction of new material was impeccable. The lesson lasted only 20 minutes. There were no machines and no individualized tasks but the teacher created an atmosphere in which the target language was, for that time, the natural medium of communication, and in which the children had a considerable degree of control over what they did and what they said. The target language was sustained throughout and, while the exchanges seemed totally natural, the language context was, in fact, carefully controlled.

Thus a similar, almost identical, foreign language methodology resulted in two very different lessons, both successful in teaching the foreign language, both contributing to the general education of the children and both marked by the sustained attentiveness of the children. The understanding of methodology, and the understanding of the specific requirements of the children, were both fully in evidence in both lessons. Both teachers, in addition, were proficient in the language, which will not be the case in all situations. The question thus arises as to how far training and experience in foreign language methodology and special education methodology can make up for deficiencies in language competence. Observation suggests that teachers underestimate what they can do with a limited corpus of language, and that training in foreign language methodology would give them the confidence to exploit fully their knowledge of the foreign language. (As part of any inservice support, teachers could be given the opportunity to work with audio-tapes to improve their own fluency, accent and accuracy. This, in fact, might be a more profitable and acceptable use of audio-tapes than using them in the classroom, since teachers still seem to find them of varying quality.)

## Methodological expertise

The optimistic belief of linguists of the 60's that a second language could be acquired in the classroom by a sort of osmosis, by the repetition of listening and speaking, or even (*pace* Chomsky) by the spontaneous activating of grammatical competence, is now no more than a canard. Apart from the limited degree of motivation and exposure, it seems that children of 11+ do not have the infant's initial grammatical competence postulated by Chomsky. Linguistic material has to be carefully chosen and presented to the children in a structured way, though the criteria for such structuring and choice are perhaps not universally agreed. These choices, moreover, are likely to be different in the special school classroom from those of the mainstream foreign language teacher. While their leisure interests may be similar, children in special schools will differ in degree from their mainstream peers in their capacity to internalize structures, in their capacity to infer and transfer, and in their long- and short-term memory. To this extent, the comments of some special school teachers, that there is no ready-made course available, have some truth in them. But this does not mean that special school teachers have to reinvent the wheel.

Children with learning difficulties are eager and enthusiastic learners in the modern language classroom. The small size of the groups enables every child who is able and willing to do so to take an active part in the learning process. It may appear thus that no special methodologies or strategies are necessary in order to hold their attention and to encourage participation: a relatively poor methodological approach may succeed where such an approach would fail disastrously with a normal class size in a mainstream school. This particular advantage of the special school may induce a complacency with regard to method; once the initial attraction of novelty begins to wane, much greater demands will be made on these teachers to sustain the motivation of the children.

Many of the teachers involved in the project are already aware of the specificities of modern language methodology, whether from their own training as language teachers, or from their reading or their experimentation in the classroom. This last is a slow and painful way of acquiring successful classroom practice, and a greater awareness is needed of the work that has already been done in this area. In particular, the exemplary methodology formulated for the early stages of the Nuffield *En Avant* scheme, for children of 7+ and for non-specialist teachers, suggests itself as the model for this situation. The material was developed for primary children and so would match the needs of secondary pupils with a delay in development. While some of the language content and some of the activities of the Nuffield scheme might need modifying for older children, it would be difficult to improve on the coherent and detailed guidance to the teacher which was presented in this course.

**Review of initial findings**

The findings of the second evaluation of the project gave no reason to question the positive conclusions of the first evaluation, although, as indicated, some thought needs to be given to the teachers' methodological expertise.

The study of a modern foreign language has perhaps a unique role to play in the fostering of positive attitudes towards a foreign culture. The presentation of aspects of *'civilisation'* formed part of the programme in most of the schools from the beginning, ranging from a French assembly, a French lunch or a French day in the school, to contacts with similar schools in France, a day-trip to France and even, in one case, a camping expedition in France. (During this project children took it in turns to buy the day's supplies from the camp shop, which was run by a monolingual Frenchman).

Teachers have become more confident in developing whole school events as the value of the modern language programme has been established. Learning a foreign language can contribute to the confidence and self-esteem of children in special schools: they can be given some responsibility for their own learning and their participation in the group; they can be given a sense of achievement in clearly defined tasks, which can be as modest as an appropriate response to a specific situation; short-and long-term memory may be improved; aural and visual discrimination are guided and fostered; bodily and facial expressiveness are developed; and, not least, an open and enquiring attitude to a different culture can be acquired.

There was a marked improvement in the quality and amount of material used in the lessons and available to the children: this was no doubt largely due to teachers' experience of what was useful and successful, but also to a grant for materials from the local authority to each participating school. Teachers had bought display boards and attractive visual aids; children's picture books and dictionaries; French language games; course material intended for low ability mainstream children. The teachers' home-made material was also generally attractive, clear and unambiguous. Most had found Mary Glasgow Publications a useful source of suitable material, and some knew of European Schoolbooks. They were also selecting non-culture-specific aids from their general language development materials. A consensus seemed to be emerging to use *Eclair* as the basic course material instead of the *Niveau Seuil* material used initially.

Teacher expectation of the children had in many cases improved, most markedly in the instances observed of good practice. Where good methodological practice ensured firm acquisition of structures and lexical items, the children's confidence and spontaneity were encouraged; this in turn enabled the teacher to make greater demands on the individual pupil.

It is perhaps still too early to make a definitive prognosis regarding the children's progress, and most teachers seem to be thinking no further than Level 2. There is certainly no loss of enthusiasm among children who have been learning French for two or more years, and while there were in most cases clear signs of progress in language acquisition, the increase in confidence and self-assurance was even more marked. The children's language performance and potential would indicate that the identification and recognition of short-term goals (perhaps linked to the National Curriculum Levels) and the possible provision of a second foreign language, as suggested in the first report, are still appropriate. Some teachers advocated language 'modules' interspersed with breaks, a scheme which would accommodate one or more foreign languages; others emphasized the importance of continuity, which would indicate a single foreign language as recommended in the proposals.

The most marked change in the two years of the pilot scheme appeared in teacher attitudes and in their conception of the contribution of a modern foreign language to the special school curriculum. Although the language content in lessons was still primarily referential and instrumental, few teachers now defined their principal aims as being purposeful communication in an authentic (i.e. French) context. They spoke of increasing the children's confidence; of enabling them to make a fresh start in a new area, without a previous history of failure; of the formation of acceptable attitudes towards a different language, culture and people; of the pleasure of the experience. No doubts were now expressed as to the ability of children to cope with this new learning experience, and teachers and headteachers spoke eloquently of the general educational benefits. It was clear that foreign language teachers can now rely on the unqualified support of headteachers, other members of staff and parents. Another change was apparent in the commitment of teachers to this area of the curriculum; many had increased the proportion of their teaching time given to the foreign language.

It still seemed to the present writers, however, that insufficient attention was being directed to what has been referred to as the 'ludic' aspects of language; games, rhymes, songs, drama (for example, in only one school, it seemed, were puppets used in language lessons; in one other the teacher used video to record the children's role-play). The National Curriculum document 'Modern Foreign Languages in the National Curriculum' (November 1991) again emphasizes the importance of this aspect of children's school experience (Area G: The World of Imagination and Creativity, p. 29). Most teachers seemed aware of these possibilities in the modern foreign language classroom, though perhaps uncertain as to how to incorporate them in their teaching. This may be rather surprising, given that this type of activity would normally be part of the methodological '*bagages*' of the special school teacher.

A high level of proficiency in language is not a *sine qua non* in this context; a supportive in-service programme, confidence in using modern foreign language methodology and a reasonable variety of attractive teaching materials are more important. During the pilot study the teachers were brought together on a monthly basis to discuss activities and to plan new projects, and this support is now continuing under the guidance of the advisory team. The teachers are looking into the use of information technology and appropriate audio-visual materials. This type of support has been commended by the Working Group (*2:Chap. 17*).

Given the doubts expressed at the time of the first evaluation regarding the provision of foreign language teachers, it was reassuring to find a substantial number who had been involved in the scheme from its inception, and interesting to note that in many cases they had increased the proportion of their time given to teaching the modern foreign language. In one of the instances of good practice quoted above the teacher is working on the production of course material for French in special schools. In the other example the French teacher is also the Music specialist, and is developing an integrated approach. She had also initiated a 'cascade' system, giving lead lessons in the presence of less experienced colleagues, who then taught their own classes.

These are the teachers whose contribution to an in-service programme would be invaluable: their competence, their commitment and enthusiasm could not fail to inform and inspire their colleagues. Add to this Berkshire's energetic and equally committed teacher adviser, and the prognosis can only be positive.

### Areas of experience

The final orders were published towards the end of the second evaluation. Some of the suggested activities from the areas of experience (*1:pp. 27–31*) most appropriate for special schools have been listed below under the headings proposed in the orders. The orders give examples of the range of experience advocated: everyday experience, personal and social life, the world around us, preparation for adult life, the use of communication, the international world and the world of imagination and creativity.

The special school with its smaller team of teachers should be able to provide opportunities to develop modern language work across the curriculum by interweaving opportunities into a range of subject activities. Some will arise naturally: most kitchens use French recipes; mathematical activities, map work or the use of French words for describing and labelling colour can widen the child's experience within the normal curriculum. Children' s progress can be recorded on a class cassette or a video.

*Communicating in the target language*

The suggestions in the orders emphasize the use of language for a wide range of purposes. Even in the early stages there is a need, for example, to provide opportunities for role play and the expression of personal feelings. Pupils should not become passive learners but be encouraged to ask about meanings, to seek clarification or repetition.

*Understanding and responding*

The orders encourage the provision of different types of spoken language: songs, rhymes, poems and plays. They list some examples of written texts such as signs, notices, postcards, letters, diaries, using authentic materials wherever possible. Where schools have made links with a school in France the acquisition of such material will be easier.

*Developing language skills and the awareness of language*

In schools with a multi-ethnic population there are already opportunities for children to recognize the existence of a range of languages. There is opportunity for raising the esteem of the child with a minority home language who is already bilingual, and to provide a real learning situation. Consideration can be given to adopting one of the home languages as an option for study within the school. This would enable a greater number of children with severe learning difficulties to be included in the modern language groups as they will already have familiarity with two languages.

Rhymes, songs, jokes and tongue twisters have a ready appeal to children and can be used to develop the patterns and rhythms of the new language.

*Developing cultural awareness*

Where schools can create links with schools in France this will form the basis of real experience. An appeal to the local community may bring native speakers into the special school to support the work.

*Developing the ability to work with others*

Opportunities for cooperation will arise both in language work, when children practise their new phrases, and in the preparation of materials for a creative activity or a simple survey. It is possible, for example, for children with knowledge of 'Quel âge as-tu?' and numbers to investigate the age profile of a class and to produce a French rather than an English histogram.

*Developing the ability to learn independently*

Computer activities, audio-cassettes and video-recorders and cameras offer opportunities for the children to work more independently and for them to record their own progress.

The following extract from a CILT project bulletin (4) emphasizes the wide range of skills that can be developed by the modern language programme:

> Working in collaboration with another curriculum area brings many benefits to both the teacher and learner. Teachers can plan and evaluate programmes of work together to avoid duplication and ensure consolidation of skills, knowledge and concepts. Learners are invited to bring their own experiences and interests into the modern languages classroom and, similarly, take what they have learned there into another curriculum area. The statements that follow are taken from the National Curriculum.

*These activities contribute to the curriculum by developing in pupils:*

> *listening skills and sensitivity to sounds;*
>
> *self-motivation, self-discipline, self-analysis and self-evaluation;*
>
> *communication skills (verbal and non-verbal), awareness of a wide range of cultural traditions;*
>
> *study skills, including attention to detail, accuracy, memorizing and the interpretation of sound and symbols;*
>
> *the ability to analyse and solve problems;*
>
> *social skills, such as cooperation, resourcefulness, perseverance, tolerance and self-confidence;*
>
> *delight in a sense of individual and collective achievement;*
>
> *imagination and inventiveness;*
>
> *aesthetic appreciation and discrimination.*

They have been taken not from a foreign languages document, but from the National Curriculum Music Working Group Interim Report.

**Long live languages and music for all!**

---

(4) *CILT: Languages and Special Educational Needs Project Bulletin, n.d.*

# References

Allen, E. D. and Vallette. R. M. (1972) *Modern language classroom techniques: a handbook*. New York: Harcourt Brace Jovanovich.

Allen, E. D. and Vallette, R. M. (1997) *Classroom techniques in foreign language and English as a second language*. New York: Harcourt Brace Jovanovich.

Altman, H. B. and James, C. V. (1979) *Foreign language teaching: meeting individual needs*. Oxford: Pergamon Press.

Arestein, J. (1956) *Ronds, Traits, Points*. Paris: Nathan.

Cole, L. R. (1973) *Language teaching in action*. London: Longman.

Corder, S. P. (1966) *The visual element in language teaching*. London: Longman.

Hodgson, F. M. (1976) *Learning modern languages. London: Library Association (London and Home Counties Branch)*.

Lee, W. R. (1979) *Language teaching games and contests*. Oxford: Oxford University Press.

Lee, W. R. and Coppen, H. (1964) *Simple audio-visual aids to language teaching*. Oxford: Oxford University Press.

Lonergan, J. (1984) *Video in language teaching*. Cambridge: Cambridge University Press.

Nuffield Foundation (1977) *The early teaching of modern languages*. London: Nuffield Foundation.

Rowlands, D. (ed) (1972) *Group-work in modern languages*. York: University of York.

Wright, A. *et al*. (1984) *Games for language learning*. Cambridge: CUP.

N.B. Most of these titles appeared at the time of the Primary French experiment. However, they are still valid pedagogically and contain sound suggestions for the development of a specific methodology for teaching modern foreign languages to children with special educational needs.

# CHAPTER 7

# *Art*

*Rod Taylor*

> Within the generality of special needs in art and design education, *all* SEN
> pupils benefit from: *recognition* of differences, and the matching of
> appropriate activities to individual educational needs; *opportunities* to
> develop their abilities at their own pace; and *support* at individual teacher and
> institution level to nurture self-esteem by helping them experience success.
> (*Art Interim Report*)

## 1. Introduction and context

There are dramatic implications for the special educational needs sector in
the recommendations of the Art Working Group in the *Interim* and *Art for
ages 5 to 14* reports, and the subsequent NCC modifications. Few would
argue with the above quotation, but low expectations can still militate
against the development of 'self-esteem'; as one Wigan teacher working in
the special needs sector summarises the problem, many 'see the handicap
before the child.' Art, with its fusions of thought and feeling, is a
fundamental, universal mode of expression and communication of the
utmost relevance in this respect. It is to the detriment of *all* children
educated in the last few years that the disciplines which systematically
facilitate expression of personal thought and feeling – the arts – were
invariably squeezed into inadequate timetable slots as other subjects with
enhanced National Curriculum clout came on stream. The Art Working
Group's proposals with their resource implications, time included, have
wide-ranging implications for all pupils, including those in the special needs
sector.

Art becomes a foundation subject in September 1992 – the last, along
with PE and Music. The *Interim Report* was published in February 1991,

and the group's final document, *Art for ages 5 to 14*, early in the Autumn Term. Draft Orders were published on 27 January 1992 and NCC non-statutory guidance is due on 4 March. Considerable changes in government thinking and attitudes have taken place since the first core subjects – already modified – were introduced, the Secretary of State belatedly heeding warnings of curriculum overcrowding. This has been to the detriment of Art and Music, perhaps simply because they were still to come on stream – though there were always suspicions that the sequencing of core and foundation subjects indicated a three-tier system, core subjects at the top, lesser foundation ones at the bottom, the order of introduction indicating perceived subject importance. The Secretary of State announced his intention to make Art optional at key stage 4 in January 1991. The *Interim Report* stressed 'the central role played by training in art and design in the promotion of visual literacy and in equipping pupils with the ability to 'read' and evaluate images. This we regard as a central part of the education that will enable them to cope knowledgeably and competently with the modern world. For this reason we are ... firmly of the view that art should remain a foundation subject within the National Curriculum for the age range 14 to 16 as much as for younger pupils.' Would this influence government thinking at the consultation stage?

## 2. A holistic view of Art for all?

The Art Working Group emphasised a holistic view of the subject: 'We consider the processes of art and design to be integrated and holistic ... In teasing out the various strands of the processes, our purpose was not to separate them from each other, but rather to understand better the way they interact within an indivisible whole.' They proposed three attainment targets in the *Interim Report* which, the Secretary of State having requested one word titles (but that they consider reducing three to two), became AT1, Understanding; AT2, Making; and AT3, Investigating – the Group reaffirming its commitment to the three.

One paragraph, 3.26, is devoted to special educational needs in the *Interim Report*, expanded to four, 11.6–11.9, in the chapter 'Art for all' in *Art for ages 5 to 14*. There is irony in the chapter title itself, for the document, like that for music, excludes reference to the 14 to 16 age band represented in all other core and foundation subject documents. The Secretary of State chose the middle of the consultation period on whether Art and Music should be optional to stipulate in the *Parent's Charter* the right of young people *not* to study them, thus undermining by pre-determining its outcome the whole consultation exercise; 'to be parading it in the Parent's Charter as though it is a benefit is an outrage', stated Professor Ken Robinson in the *TES* of 4 October, 1991. The notion of the broad and balanced curriculum promised for all pupils in the Education

Reform Act was dented; an essential area of human experience – the aesthetic – present in every entitlement curriculum document of the last decade, was now no longer an essential part of all young people's entitlement!

## 3. The aesthetic dimension

The National Curriculum had failed, from the outset, to take any adequate account of the arts as a whole, subsuming some within other disciplines – drama and dance, as well as verbal arts – and tagging others – dance within PE plus art and music – on at the end, almost as an afterthought. Having made Art and Music optional, there were then ministerial suggestions that the aesthetic could be picked up elsewhere but, given the construction of the National Curriculum, they presented the only *guarantees* of the aesthetic being addressed at *every* key stage. Art and Music are primarily concerned with the aesthetic, whereas non-arts subjects, at best, touch upon aesthetic matters only in passing; note the technology debate with many traditional CDT practitioners only able to conceive of the aesthetic as a belated afterthought to 'tart' up the appearance of what are frequently ill-designed functional objects to begin with!

The word 'aesthetic' originally came into the English language to denote forms of knowing to do with *apprehension through the senses*, relating both to responses to nature and to works of art created by human beings 'with intention' and of relevance to life issues. Subsequently, the word became associated with taste, refinement and elegance, taking on much narrower elitist connotations. It is this aspect, unfortunately, which *Art for ages 5 to 14* emphasises: 'Here, aesthetic is taken to indicate the principles of taste in art: the study of beauty and, to a lesser extent, of its opposite, the ugly' (p. 55). This is unfortunate as the document goes a long way towards establishing a model of art education with potential to develop children's abilities to apprehend through the senses – of the utmost relevance across the whole special needs spectrum, whereas taste and beauty, divorced from their proper basis in sensory experience, are likely to be of little or no relevance. Aesthetic and artistic 'knowing' embraces both verbal and non-verbal means; an art vocabulary is often seen as signifying the practical elements of colour, line, texture and tone – examples abound in both reports – but acquisition and use of a verbal language developed through significant art experiences is equally essential, and likewise requires careful cultivation.

## 4. Making activities

Traditionally, art education has been concerned with making activities, invariably to the exclusion of all other aspects. AT2 provides the central backbone of both reports, with examples covering the full fine art, design continuum with the words 'art, craft and design' consciously used throughout *Art for ages 5 to 14*. Art was the word used in the Education Reform Act, seemingly borne of an ignorance of the subject and its history, all GCSE subject examinations and higher education courses, for example, being in 'art and design'. The report emphasises the importance of craft skills and refers to the significance of art and design activities to Technology; a section demonstrating the importance of art to technology in gender terms would not have come amiss, however, given the wide range of gender-free design and technological activities practised by boys and girls across the Art 2D, 3D, textiles spectrum, and the gender bias still inherent in much technology practice.

There is a regrettable vagueness about the end of key stage statements in *Art for ages 5 to 14*. They do not provide an adequate basis for assessment, the looseness of some words and phrases actually being potentially harmful. For example, by the end of KSI in AT2, pupils should have demonstrated that they can 'work practically and imaginatively with a limited range of materials and tools . . .' It is surely not too much to ask that these children should have had experience of working 'in 2D, 3D and textiles media and processes'. Once stipulated, this could certainly be realised; in other curriculum areas the National Curriculum makes significant new demands. Overall, the Art documents do so as well, but words like *limited* condone existing bad practice and affirm low expectations.

## 5. Broadening the art curriculum

Both documents take account of the major subject developments of recent years. The belief that art and design education should develop pupils' critical and discriminative powers, help them to become visually alert, and to understand the functions of art within society and culture is by no means new, but it is only in the last decade that examples of theory being effectively translated into classroom practice have arisen. The logical outcome of these developments is that all children should be educated to enjoy and know about the art of others as well as making their own, with both activities seen as interdependent, nurturing and enriching each other. There is now a considerable body of practice illustrating how pupils' work can develop in unexpected but dynamic ways through their knowledge informing their making. Equally, motivated attitudes towards the art of others can intensify because of the relevance it now assumes in relation to their own work.

The Group's three attainment target model went a long way towards providing critical and practical criteria for course construction throughout the key stages, opening up – for the first time – the genuine possibility of an art education in which continuity and progression could be seriously addressed from five to sixteen. Even though the document's title was restricted to 5 to 14, the implications for GCSE Art are considerable (about 40 per cent of pupils currently study the subject to that level). The critical studies dimensions bring with them tangible criteria for assessment in terms of language development through art experiences and for pupils assessing their own practice and development in relation to their insights into the art of others. An ever-evolving understanding of art provides a necessary basis for gauging one's own progress whilst increasing the range of practical possibilities.

## 6. Some negative arguments

At the consultation stage of the *Interim Report*, concerns were expressed about AT1; the most challenging changes for *all* teachers and schools are to be found here. Critical studies approaches can still raise fears about children been prevented from 'simply' enjoying art, and the AT1 end of key stage statements made constant reference to talking, describing, reading and use of an appropriate and 'developed art vocabulary'. Special needs – as if there were one universal special need – became a focus for this argument; surely these children should just be allowed to enjoy themselves! One can have *some* sympathy for this argument in a climate where over-riding concerns appear to be those of using national curriculum testing to make child compete with child, school with school, and authority with authority, allied to a seemingly irrevocable move towards paper and pencil testing, in spite of its obvious limitations and the inevitable narrowing of the curriculum it creates. However, without possession of even the most basic art vocabulary, pupils cannot negotiate about their own art, or that of others, at even the most rudimentary level. Rather than the pupil simply enjoying art, it is extremely frustrating to be unneccessarily restricted in forming concepts or entering into appropriate dialogue with teacher or peers. *All* pupils should be helped to acquire an art vocabulary commensurate with their age, stage of development, ability and intelligence as a *basic necessity* of art education – 'the limits of my language are the limits of my world', declared Jerome Bruner.

This does not mean writing art history essays and learning dates and facts instead of producing paintings, sculptures or textile works: far from it! It means teachers consciously helping children develop and extend their vocabularies by whatever means appropriate. Much of this should obviously take place in interactive ways during the actual course of practical activities or through direct engagements with original art works. Pupils benefiting from such an education testify to its relevance, for it is relatively uncommon within most school contexts for them to be required to use language expressive of both thoughts and feelings, and it is in this combination that an art vocabulary gains special relevance. We are failing children where this fundamental right is denied, on whatever grounds.

Surely *all* children should be helped to fulfil their potential in this area, and the National Curriculum opens up extensive and fruitful possibilities.

The *Interim Report* is much stronger in this respect than its successor with regard to the end of key stage statements. In AT1 in *Art for ages 5 to 14* every single reference to talk, discussion, etc. has disappeared. Did those citing special needs as the basis for their 'enjoyment' argument exert undue influence on the Working Group? Allied to this, of course, is the deep-rooted fear that AT1 demands that teachers must also extend *their* knowledge of art and artists, as some are constantly doing already. Many strategies exist now, though, to facilitate children's direct engagement with a wide variety of art works, as opposed to passively receiving the opinions of 'experts' about a set range of European works taught in chronological sequence. Within the resulting interactive contexts, pupils frequently develop the desire to find out more through further enquiries, including reading and voluntary gallery visiting – the once prevalent myth that children needed 'protection' from the influences of adult art in order to preserve their natural creativity and spontaneity has now been completely exploded.

## 7. NCC modifications

When the NCC *Consultation Report on Art* was published in January 1992, it came as no surprise that only two ATs were specified, even though 63 per cent of responses to *Art for ages 5 to 14* were in favour of three and only 10 per cent against. AT1 now becomes Investigating and Making, and AT2 Knowledge and Understanding. Study of different cultures and artistic traditions is emphasised but, as with Music, the naming of specific European art movements and periods to be studied has led to heated controversy, with suggestions that this, within a two AT context, will create a 50:50 divide between theory and practice. Close scrutiny does not support this argument, there being 44 PoS in AT1 and only 25 in AT2, of which 6 relate directly to the pupil's own practice. In fact, there are additions with nothing lost to the point where NCC can be seen as having the equivalent of four ATs instead of the three! Equally important, musicians are vociferously arguing that the requirement that pupils study the music of the past is retrogressive – it is through making their own music that children *know*. 'Child Music' rarely developed, but around thirty years of 'Child Art' emphatically underlined that making alone produces, at best, only limited knowledge – hence the reappraisals of the last decade and a now widespread acceptance that children must also be systematically introduced to the art of others.

NCC makes no stipulations about depth of study required, or how specified periods and movements are addressed, leaving exciting scope for further critical studies developments. So long as arid art history teaching does not become the norm, there are great possibilities for the contextualisation of practical projects, with non-specialist teachers now having necessary criteria to help them acquire resources. Likewise, in-depth exploration of broad-based themes – the changing landscape, the human form, etc. – provide scope for works from every specified movement and period at KS2 and 3 to be naturally introduced and addressed in ways beneficial to practice while making the knowledge acquired more personally relevant. Much is being made of the resource implications, but a minimum requirement would be that each practical topic or project be supported by reproductions representing pertinent examples from each specified period or movement – a by no means impossible imposition!

## 8. Special Needs and a broadened art curriculum

*Art for ages 5 to 14* emphasized that 'art education can make a valuable contribution to pupils with special educational needs (physical, sensory, emotional and behavioural)' and that 'they can derive much benefit from working with a range of materials, media and processes which can help to develop positive attitudes' (11.6) The document stresses the need for pupils to be able 'to show what they have achieved, by whatever means appropriate'. (11.7) This is in keeping with the GCSE criterion that pupils should be assessed on what they *know, understand and can do*, a principle currently in danger of being lost sight of. There is a need to look at alternative means of giving access to the art curriculum through, for example, 'the use of computers, physical aids or the provision of special assistance'. In order to ensure the safe handling of tools, materials and equipment 'the adaptation of work spaces and equipment may need to be considered' while provision required to support 'language-related work' is also emphasised. That a critical art vocabulary should be consciously cultivated in relation to capabilities here as elsewhere has already been emphasized, with pupils encouraged to engage with art works, considering such aspects as their content, form, process and mood. Each aspect can stimulate different types of response and, in the process, encourage use of different types of language, some art-specific, but with much having potential for general usage.

Finally, in 11.9, the benefits of out-of-school activities are addressed, with specified appropriate venues including sculpture and wildlife parks, potteries and artists' studios. Strangely, though, art galleries are mentioned not in their own right but only with regard to outreach work, implying that the more confined spaces of the gallery are unsuitable for special needs groups. Outstanding practice already takes place, however; systematic use of the Royal Academy 'Monet in the '90's' exhibition by physically handicapped pupils was of particular note given the vast numbers attending that exhibition! The Drumcroon Education Art Centre in Wigan, an extremely compact venue, consistently accommodates special needs groups of all categories, while the case study featuring maladjusted children recorded in *Educating for Art* (Rod Taylor, 1986, Longman) provides classic testimony of those children benefiting through exposure to art works encountered in the original and shows how this, in turn, motivated their whole approach to learning.

Evidence from the USA (*Artists-in-Schools: Analysis and Criticism*, 1978) indicates that school-based artists often have little contact with special needs pupils. Norma Tait, a member of the Artists in Wigan Schools Scheme, requested that she work in the special needs sector in 1987 (see *Artists in Wigan Schools*, Rod Taylor, 1991, Gulbenkian Foundation). She effectively demonstrates that when expectations are high, achievements can be extraordinary: 'Each person is special. I think everybody has got special needs – all of us.' Norma sees the child before the handicap and, in the process, illustrates the vast untapped potential there to be developed. Working in close partnership with an equally gifted teacher, both provide opportunities for pupils to develop their skills, some actually obtaining success at GCSE level where previously no prospects had existed for them. With the reduced of local authority personnel and resources, the capacity for special needs pupils to benefit so positively from these essential resources needs strongly asserting in the current climate.

Art should become more varied and broadly-based in the future, if National Curriculum recommendations become reality. The NCC *Consultation Report* states that the Art proposals 'will (with necessary modifications) be suitable for pupils with SEN.' Such modifications should be determined by positive criteria like those written into Wigan's *Arts in Schools Policy Statement* (Wigan Education Department, 1991), with regard to special educational needs in the Arts:

(i) A range of opportunities commensurate with their needs and abilities should be on offer to all pupils rather than disabilities become the basis for limitation or restriction of experience.

(ii) All pupils are individuals and, as such, can be seen as having special needs, gifts and talents which have to be met in order that they realise their full potential.

(iii) Disability as such should not be the basis for denial of access to the Arts and their varied forms.

As an entitlement right, pupils with SEN should share as fully as possible all the benefits of the more broadly-based art education about to be introduced, with their art making informed by their increased knowledge and understanding, both aspects being equally carefully cultivated and developed in interactive ways because each is crucial to any worthwhile education in the subject.

# CHAPTER 8

# PE: Movement in the Right Direction

*David A. Sugden*

The Physical Education Working Group was established in July 1990 and submitted an interim report to the Secretaries of State in December 1990 outlining their thoughts on attainment targets and programmes of study. The Secretaries of State expressed concern about some of the report particularly about the original recommended structure of three attainment targets, choice of activity in key stages 3 and 4, residential experience, resource implications and unnecessary jargon. The revised document reviewed here, *Physical Education for ages 5 to 16*, addresses these and other issues only partially covered in the interim report. Special educational needs is one of the issues which was mentioned in the Interim Report, but little detail was provided. In the revised Report, the Working Party has firmly tackled special educational needs setting out sound principles coupled with some guidance.

Physical education draws upon a wide audience of interested professionals such as PE associations, governing bodies of sports, national and regional sports and arts councils, and dance associations, all anxious that their particular interests be represented in the National Curriculum. This placed considerable demands upon the Working Party. It is also a subject containing diverse activities, such as dance, canoeing, hockey, throwing the discus etc., which can be organised and structured in a number of different ways. The Working Group wisely resisted the temptation to structure the attainment target(s) by activities, and opted for the more logical thematic approach.

In the Report, the rationale for physical education in the curriculum is divided into two parts with several components each. First there is the unique/special contribution that physical education makes in educating young people through the use of the body and its movements. This includes the development of physical competence, promoting physical development and its benefits, developing artistic understanding, and the establishment of self-esteem through the development of self confidence in competitive and cooperative situations. Secondly, physical education also contributes to the development of problem solving skills, the development of interpersonal skills, and the forging of links between the school and the community and across cultures. Alongside the rationale, is the notion that equal opportunities is a cross curricular dimension and, in physical education,

> means that all children should be allowed access to and given confidence in the different activities involved, regardless of their ability, sex or cultural/ethnic background. (page 15)

A core part of the PE National Curriculum is the single attainment target (AT) with a main emphasis of **participation** reflecting the active nature of the subject, but should also encompass the **planning** and **evaluation** of activities. In the Interim Report these three – planning, participating and evaluating were three separate attainment targets, but the Secretary of State asked the group to reconsider with a view to having one AT stressing the active nature of the subject. The present report reflects this while still keeping the valuable processes of planning and evaluating, which are now incorporated into the participation attainment target.

The Working Party has tried to keep the natural advantage that physical education has with respect to the developing child. The motor development of children, while not progressing in distinct stages, can be described in general phases. In the first two years of life the baby is gaining control of posture, locomotion and manipulation. At birth the baby has movements which are divided into those which are reflexive and those which are spontaneous, many of which disappear, or merge into voluntary control. By two years of age the child is competent in locomotion and has a wide range of adaptable manipulative skills with which to interact with the environment. Between two and six or seven years of age, children develop the locomotor skills of running, jumping, hopping, skipping, catching, throwing, climbing etc., plus a repertoire of manual skills including writing and drawing.

One could make the argument that after the age of seven, children do not naturally develop any new skills: they simply refine, combine, adapt, create, mix, play with the skills they already possess. Between seven years and puberty there is a stable growth period for children, with predictable increments each year. It is also a period when other processes appear which are crucial to the solving of movement problems. Thus the child reacts much faster, is better at predicting and anticipating, and develops a number of cognitive strategies all of which contribute to the child being more competent in situations which are unpredictable (Keogh & Sugden, 1985).

The implications from this would be a broad-based curriculum in the first two years with children gaining a vocabulary of movement skills from which they can move confidently into more specific activities, such as the various sports forms.

The PE National Curriculum proposals have used this natural progression in many of their levels of attainment and end of key stage statements, and in the programmes of study. For key stages 1 and 2, six areas of activity are to be covered – athletic activities, dance, games, gymnastic activities, outdoor and adventurous activities and swimming. Swimming is not required in key stage 3, although an end of key stage 2 statement is that children should be able to swim at least 25 metres and demonstrate an understanding of water safety. At key stage 4 all pupils not undertaking GCSE in PE should study at least two activities which can be from different or same areas.

Thus the Report tries to take a developmental perspective with younger children being immersed in a wide range of motor activities with a concentration on variety. For example in the Programmes of Study for key stage 1 it is recommended that 'children should experience and develop a wide range of movements many of which occur in more than one activity'. (page 29) In key stage 2 'children's motor skills, control and coordination develop greatly and the programme of work in Physical Education should help and refine these' (page 30). These are then utilized in sport and dance type activities, with an increasing specificity. For example 'In key stage 3 pupils should continue to learn more specific forms of activities through carefully planned series of lessons' (page 32). Finally, in key stage 4, children are asked to make choices such that they can specialise in certain activities with a view to these becoming lifelong recreational pursuits.

Two parts of the report make particular reference to children with special educational needs. Appendix A expands upon some early statements about descriptions and principles. A distinction is made between children who have statements under the 1981 Education Act and may or may not have movement difficulties, and those who are not the subject of a statement but may have special educational needs in a PE lesson. A distinction is then made between **impairment, disability** and **handicap. Impairment** is when the child has a defective limb, organ or mechanism of the body or missing a limb. **Disability** implies that there is some functional loss because of this impairment, and **handicap** occurs when the child is disadvantaged by this, such as in restriction of ability or access. These are useful distinctions to make because it is clear that a child can be impaired and/or disabled, but not handicapped, and this can be helpful when different interpretations and adaptations to the programme are being planned.

The Report outlines four principles for a physical education programme for children with special educational needs. The first principle is that of **entitlement**, which repeats the now well known phrase that all children are entitled to the National Curriculum, which may need modification for this entitlement to occur. The second principle of **access** follows directly from the first, and is achieved in a number of ways. The Report notes that programmes of study, end of key stage statements, and non-statutory levels of attainment are so stated that as few modifications as possible need to be made. But where modifications are required then they ought to be done. The third principle is one of **integration** with children showing disabilities participating alongside their able-bodied peers if possible without altering the activity. If this is not possible, modifying rules or equipment should be explored in order to facilitate integration. They note that only after all options like this have been tried should **segregation** or **substitution** take place and that this should be very rare. In the Report the term 'segregation' means taking part in the same activity as their able bodied peers, but with the activity modified and with the pupils separated from their colleagues. By 'substitution' the Report means that children take part in some other activity altogether but still part of the National Curriculum in physical education. The report notes that able bodied children will benefit from sharing lessons with their disabled peers, enabling them to appreciate their contributions and achievements. The fourth principle is that activities which have been modified or substituted must have **integrity**, with no place for activities which are trivial, have no educational content, which are demeaning or require too little effort on the part of the pupils.

These four principles provide a backcloth for other issues which the Report raises. It stresses the need for partnership in extending an understanding of disabilities and advises that it may be necessary to develop links with parents, therapists and other professionals from the educational and medical fields. The Report also states that physical education has an important role to play in therapy for all children with special educational needs even though this may not be a primary role, which is still 'to help develop motor competence and confidence in the physical and social self' (page 57). Physical education will have a particular therapeutic value for children with profound and multiple learning difficulties, inserting the provocative statement that for these children it is probably the most important subject on the curriculum. The Report is very firm when it states 'National Curriculum physical education must not be disapplied for these children' (page 57). There is value in obtaining a breadth of physical experience through it and there should be formal ways of recording the progress. Finally the Report makes a recommendation that links between special and mainstream schools should be extended, and that all schools with children with special educational needs in physical education should develop links with local sports organisations and clubs for people with disabilities, with the possibility that for some children activities in key stage 4 could be offered through these organisations.

Included in Section 9 of the Report are the programmes of study for pupils with special educational needs. This starts by noting that the four principles above should underpin any programme of physical education, and then offers some guidelines for teachers in mainstream schools who have children with special needs in physical education in their classes. It is noted that this is less detailed than is desirable, stressing the need to look for additional help.

The Report offers a short paragraph of guidelines for the teaching of physical education across a number of population groups. The following are examples from these:

- For children with hearing impairments teachers are advised to speak clearly with the light full on their face; it is noted that some of these children may also have balance problems.
- For children with visual impairments clear verbal instructions are recommended, and the use of auditory cues rather than visual may be beneficial. Modified equipment such as brightly coloured items is recommended, and the children should be encouraged to comment on their own performance as they may have difficulty in seeing the detail of other children's work.
- For children with learning difficulties the difficulty may be understanding instructions such that they can be turned into a desired action. Language which is easy to understand plus task analysis is recommended. Mention is made of particular forms of movement education such as the Sherbourne method (Sherbourne, 1990) which may be particularly advantageous for some children.
- For children with emotional and behavioural difficulties there is benefit from working in pairs and sharing space and equipment, with an emphasis on creative activities letting the children produce their own movement solutions which have been set by the teacher and not simply being told what to do. This may help in the desired move from dependent to independent learning.

The Report recognises that the group with physical impairments embraces a wide range of conditions, with the reminder that more than one disability can be present in the same child. It is good to see that the Report also recognises a group with 'no organically definable impairment, and yet who have difficulty with coordination and movement' (page 36). This group of inappropriately named 'clumsy children' are no longer the forgotten children and there is a growing body of literature covering description, identification and assessment, and intervention. (Henderson, 1987; Henderson & Hall, 1982; Laszlo & Bairstow, 1985; Sugden & Keogh, 1991). For these children the Report recommends awareness of the difficulties, appropriate task setting and reinforcement of success.

The Report includes giftedness as part of special educational needs, stressing that although outside organisations will have a major part to play, it should not be at the expense of other areas of experience for the children, and their physical education should remain the responsibility of the school, with appropriate challenges being available to them. The Report also recommends that curriculum balance is particularly important for a child who has a specific expertise in one area, and even in that area the curriculum should be able to offer a challenge.

The Report provides guideline programmes of study for children with special educational needs noting that the balance may differ for the children but because appropriate balance is not specifically spelled out for any child, it would be inappropriate to do this for children with special educational needs. Seeking help from outside agencies is encouraged, and it is noted that in at least three of the six recommended areas of study, schemes exist showing how children with disabilities can make progress in particular sports, with a cautionary note that these schemes although worthwhile are sport based and were not devised with the National Curriculum in mind.

Recommendations are given for each of the six areas of activity in an effort to ensure that the four guiding principles are fulfilled. The following selected examples provide a flavour of these. In **athletics** crutches, wheelchairs, and walking frames can be used in a number of ways to show locomotion. **Dance** is seen to make a particular contribution to children with special educational needs, with almost all children being able to respond to the proposed activities in key stage 1, such as showing moods or responding to stimuli. In **games**, modified activities are recommended together with partnership with community provision. In **gymnastic** activities some children may need support, but carefully matching tasks to the children can go a long way to ensuring access and participation. **Outdoor** and **adventure** activities are seen in a similar way to dance in that there is a special contribution to be made through the use of specialised equipment, and advice from the governing bodies of the different sports. Finally, **swimming** is an activity well known for its overall contribution to the welfare of children with special educational needs. Care over medical issues is stressed together with sensitivity over the presence of incontinence. Finally, in the programmes of study the Report stresses joint planning between professionals, special and mainstream links, and recommends that:

> every school department of physical education should have a written policy for pupils with special educational needs, which should operate within and be supported by a whole school policy. (page 39).

The end of key stage statements are broad and general such that when assessments take place, there is an allowance for flexible interpretations to accommodate children with special educational needs. In some cases the context of assessment may need to be modified or adapted such that all pupils can achieve. Examples given include swimming with aids, moving one part of the body as opposed to a total body response, and the curiously unexplained 'response to stimuli with minimal voluntary control' (page 43).

The Working Party for physical education has produced a Report which outlines a modern, logical programme of physical education. There can be some quibbles about the detail, but I believe it has produced the right structure. It has also made great efforts to take on the issue of special educational needs, certainly more than most of the other subject areas. However, a great problem exists with respect to delivery, which was not part of the Group's brief. The provision and organisation of courses in initial teacher training and INSET will be a major issue. I have a particular bias in this area, which has implications for evaluating some of the recommendations in the Report. When guidelines are given in the Report, they are usually given with respect to a particular disability such as learning difficulty or physical impairment. The problem with this is that it groups children together by disability rather than by what they need, and there is the tacit implication that these disabilities could be homogenous groupings. From these recommendations, I can see courses emerging in PE and the physically impaired, or PE and the blind, just as there are separate sports organisations for the various types of disabilities. The situation with sporting bodies is changing, but there is still some way to go.

Another approach is to start with what a teacher normally does in the gymnasium, games field, swimming pool and other activity areas and ask how this has to be changed in order to fulfill the four principles mentioned in the Report. For any child, do the instructions have to be modified? How can we do this? Will any demonstration be useful, and how can we best utilise it? How do we get the child to understand the nature of the task, what is required of him or her? How do we present feedback, and what type do we give? What is the best way to match the task with the resources of the learner? Do we change the nature of the task, by modifying and adapting or do we keep it yet break it down into smaller components? How do we break down the learning context such that the interactive nature of the task and the child is kept intact? Does the child have a difficulty with the control of the movement and what support would be useful? How are we to group children in a PE lesson? Is it better to have a range of flexible groupings according to the nature of the activity than a fixed group which remains stable? These and other questions can provide the foundations for INSET and initial teacher education courses where the emphasis is on the difficulties the child has in a PE lesson and how these difficulties can be resolved, and they go some way towards fulfilling the principles detailed in the National Curriculum Physical Education.

### References

DES (1991) *Physical Education for ages 5 to 16: proposals of the Secretary of State for Education and Science and the Secretary of State for Wales.* London: HMSO.

Henderson, S. E. & Hall, D. (1982) 'Concomitants of clumsiness in young schoolchildren'. *Developmental Medicine and Child Neurology*, **24**, 448–460.

Henderson, S. E.(1987) 'The assessment of "clumsy" children: old and new approaches'. *Journal of Child Psychology and Psychiatry and Allied Disciplines*, **28**, 511–27.

Keogh, J. F. & Sugden, D. A. (1985) *Movement skill development*. New York: Macmillan.

Laszlo, J. L. & Bairstow, P. J. (1985) *Perceptual-motor behaviour: developmental assessment and therapy*. New York: Praeger.

Sherbourne, V. (1990) *Developmental Movement For Children*. Cambridge: Cambridge University Press.

Sugden, D. A. & Keogh, J. F. (1991) *Problems in movement skill development*. Columbia: University of South Carolina Press.

# CHAPTER 9

# *Music: Striking the Right Note*

*Sean McCavera*

Chapter 4 of the Report of the Working Group on music in the National Curriculum (DES, 1991) opens with the confident assertion that 'this country will in future have a population which is better educated, musically, than ever before'. With effect from autumn 1992, music, which is a foundation subject in the National Curriculum, will, for the first time, be compulsory for all pupils in the age range of five to fourteen years. The Working Group start from the position that all pupils will benefit from music education in school and that most will be capable of following a planned and structured music curriculum in order to achieve the specified attainment targets. There is an explicit statement of the principles which extend this general position to pupils with special educational needs:

> pupils with special educational needs should be encouraged to follow the National Curriculum to the maximum extent possible; differentiation by levels of outcome as well as by the nature of tasks should allow almost all pupils with special educational needs to participate in the experiences and activities of all three attainment targets; imaginative means should be sought to enable children to achieve through their abilities, rather than being frustrated by their disabilities.

This positive approach to pupils with special educational needs is to be wholeheartedly welcomed.

## The attainment targets and their aims

The Report structures the music curriculum around three attainment targets: Performing, Composing and Appraising. This structure reflects the debate which followed publication, last December, of the interim report of the Working Group. The interim report outlined a structure of four targets, grouped into two profile components. In the scheme then proposed, Performing and Composing would have been encompassed in the profile component, Making Music, while the profile component Understanding Music would have subsumed Listening and Knowing. Since then, considerable effort has clearly been expended in clarifying notions of structure and content, so that the outline put forward for consultation (comments were invited by 1 November 1991) has an entirely defensible logic and coherence.

The Report confirms Performing and Composing as distinct and essential components of the music curriculum and emphasises that, just as performing and composing provide an active experience of music, listening is also intended to be an active and not a passive experience. Appraising is to comprise the whole process of interpretation and evaluation. There is a conscious commitment to progression in the music curriculum, so that the aim of the Report is to produce a structured framework for the development of musical skills and knowledge.

*Attainment Target 1: Performing, aims to ensure that pupils:*

- develop the skills needed to perform, both through voice work and by playing instruments;
- learn to respond appropriately to instruction and direction in music-making;
- develop confidence in presenting their performances.

The three Key Stages should offer a progression from performance of simple rhythmic and melodic patterns, to the interpretation and performance of more complex pieces. In Key Stages 1 and 2, most performances will be as part of a group; by Key Stage 3, pupils will be expected to sing or play short solo parts. Pupils should also be encouraged to exercise increasing sophistication in preparing, presenting and evaluating their performances. The Working Group recommended the use of a wide and varied repertoire to include music from different cultures and periods.

*Attainment Target 2: Composing, aims to permit pupils to:*

- develop the skills needed to devise musical compositions and arrangements;
- develop the ability to improvise;
- record their work (by notation of a score, by use of recording equipment, by use of a computer with appropriate software);
- arrange and adapt pieces.

Again, while at Key Stages 1 and 2 most of the work will be undertaken in groups, individual, as well as group work, is expected at Key Stage 3.

*Appraising, the third Attainment Target: aims to encourage the pupils to:*

- develop the skills and knowledge to respond, with understanding, to the elements of music from a range of styles and different cultural traditions;
- make reasoned judgements about, and to evaluate, performance and compositions;
- apply relevant knowledge of the historical and cultural background of the music concerned.

Pupils should learn to listen attentively, to identify, distinguish and discriminate among the elements of the music and to discuss what they have heard.

**Emphasis on practical activities**

It is the view of the members of the Working Group that music in schools should be essentially a practical activity, so that pupils' understanding and appreciation of music is to be developed through 'an active engagement in listening, performing and composing'. The curriculum is to be implemented in a way which allows pupils frequent opportunities to participate in music-making and encourages active participation.

The recommendations are framed to encourage flexibility in choice of structure and selection of content; the Report provides a set of guidelines and suggestions for action, but is deliberately not prescriptive in approach. Indeed, it is noted that 'There are ... many different styles of music, appropriate for different purposes and offering different kinds of satisfaction and challenge; excellence may be found in any style of musical expression'. In a sense, this observation encapsulates the approach of the Report as a whole - that is, the combination of the commitment to offer every pupil the opportunity to achieve the fullest and most demanding musical experience of which he or she is capable, with a refreshing openness as to the way in which this may best be achieved.

It is intended that only the attainment targets and programmes of study will be subject to statutory definition, while the more detailed statements of attainment and arrangements for assessment will be non-statutory. Assessment will, in most cases, be carried out by the music teacher only; provision for a national scheme of testing is made only for elective students at Key Stage Four. There is considerable scope for local initiative in devising an appropriate and informative format for assessment and reporting.

Those who teach music in special schools will find much which is constructive in this document. The view which informs the Report is one which recognises that 'good practice in special schools stems from teachers' recognition that access to the music curriculum is important for virtually all pupils and can be particularly so for some'.

The Working Group believes that 'every pupil who can possibly learn through the music curriculum should follow it and should where possible be integrated with other children in mainstream primary and secondary schools when doing so'. There is room for flexibility in designing programmes of study towards the attainment targets, so that the curriculum may be adapted rather than disapplied – 'what may vary in the curriculum followed by children with special needs is the balance between the three attainment targets and among the levels within them' (11.16).

### The benefits of music in special education

The Working Group argues that the study of music in schools develops a number of important and transferable skills:

- delight in a sense of individual and collective achievement;
- aesthetic appreciation and discrimination;
- listening skills and sensitivity to sounds;
- imagination and inventiveness;
- intellectual and artistic skills;
- the ability to analyse and solve problems;
- study skills, including attention to detail, lengthened attention span, concern for accuracy, memorising and the interpretation of sounds and symbols;
- communication skills (non-verbal as well as verbal);
- social skills, such as co-operation, resourcefulness, perseverance, tolerance and self-confidence;
- self-motivation, self-discipline, self-analysis and self-evaluation;
- awareness and appreciation of a wide range of cultural traditions.

All of these skills are highly relevant to children in special education; music gives a unique opportunity to develop them in a particularly effective way. The *Times Educational Supplement* recently reported (Prestage, 1991) that, apparently for the first time ever, a group from a special school for children with severe learning difficulties and severe mental and physical disabilities are to participate in the Schools Prom. The percussion band from the school has already toured in Scotland and Ireland and performed before a wide variety of audiences. There is no doubt from the photograph accompanying the article that the young performers are both experiencing a real sense of achievement and are taking great delight in that achievement!

Music not only develops the aesthetic senses, but can also be of considerable practical value in stimulating appropriate educational and personal development. All children will improve their communication and social skills through the practice of music; children with special needs may derive particular benefit from the encouragement of social skills through appropriate participation in group activities and the development of tolerance and self-discipline, for example, through learning to wait their turn.

Again, while the study of music will enable all pupils to develop listening and study skills, and to improve attention span, these are areas which will be especially rewarding for pupils with behavioural difficulties, which may hamper learning in other contexts. Music may also afford a valuable opportunity for self-expression – and for learning about appropriate means of self-expression – as well as permitting the pupil to explore personal emotions, through composition and expressive performance. We might add a number of items to the Working Group list:

- improving motor skills, through work with rhythm and percussion;
- improving general mobility through music and movement activities;
- improving alertness and concentration.

Thus, music work with children who have special needs can promote a number of aims, including the psychological and emotional, as well as the social and developmental. An emphasis on performance is particularly important, both in boosting the individual child's self-esteem and in promoting integration into the wider community. In the *TES* article on the Schools prom referred to above, Arfon Wym, headmaster of the school, says 'Parents can see a performance and be proud rather than feeling despair at having a handicapped child'.

**Examples of music teaching**

Existing arrangements for music teaching in four special schools in a North London borough offer a useful illustration of the range of provision at present. One of the schools, which has a pupil intake of children with severe learning difficulties, often associated with major physical and sensory disability, has developed close links with the Nordoff-Robbins Institute for Music Therapy. There is a regular programme of visits by therapists to the school, undertaking a combination of one-to-one and group work. In the individual sessions, the therapist will use the basic elements of music-making – rhythm, pitch and melody – to establish communication with the child. The therapist uses voice or a simple musical instrument to reach out, through sound, to the child. In an initial session a child might have to respond to a simple rhythm pattern. The child is encouraged to respond at will, vocally or instrumentally, and the therapist builds on that response to continue and develop the interaction. The approach is flexible, child-centred and non-directive. In the group sessions, the therapist encourages the children to participate jointly in a collective music-making exercise, perhaps using percussion instruments.

Music-making in a school for physically handicapped pupils gives rise to different, but no less demanding, challenges. Here, the emphasis is on participation by all pupils – even those pupils who are unable to use language are encouraged to join in by clapping, or tapping, or by making non-verbal sounds. Music teaching is provided by a combination of resources. One part-time teacher has particular responsibility for art and music in the school. There are also links with a number of local community arts groups, and projects have been undertaken with external arts groups, where music is introduced as one element of an integrated music and drama course.

Some teachers include music as a normal part of creative work on cross-curricular themes: in one example observed in the classroom, a group of pupils encountered difficulty in writing a poem on the term's theme of 'Great Lives', but were able to make much more progress when encouraged to put their words together with a rhythmic accompaniment to produce a 'rap'. Where possible, older pupils from the school are offered partial integration programmes, run jointly with a group of local further education colleges and are able to select options from a range of courses. Many choose to take music as part of a performance course or as one unit in a Certificate of Pre-Vocational Education course. Through this scheme, pupils from the school take part, with their able-bodied peers, in a structured series of music-making and composition exercises, culminating in performance at the college in a Christmas concert and a summer show.

There is some use of computers with simple music software at the school and this does afford access for some pupils who are unable, because of physical disability, to hold or manipulate musical instruments.

This generally positive experience with music is also found at a school for pupils with moderate learning difficulties. Again, the provision for music is resourced in a variety of ways, both from the school's own staff and from external groups. Music is seen as an essential ingredient in the school's commitment to positive support of cultural diversity. Thus, music is a key element of school assemblies, which aim to mark and celebrate important festivals of each major cultural and ethnic group and efforts are made to select and perform a range of pieces which reflect the variety of backgrounds represented at the school – among staff as well as pupils.

In contrast, staff at a school for boys with emotional and behavioural disturbances acknowledge that music has had to take a relatively low priority on the curriculum. This is not a matter of choice, nor does it reflect the preference of either staff or pupils, but reflects other demands on the school timetable and a lack of specialist resources at the school.

**The need for adequate resources**

There are a number of important conclusions to be drawn from this brief review of present provision in a small group of schools. There is an almost universal recognition of the value of music for pupils with special educational needs. Music teaching is perceived to play an important role in meeting the psychological needs of the pupils, in developing their capabilities of self-expression and in fostering social skills, as well as providing an arena for positive achievement and enhancement of self-esteem. It is generally and quite clearly recognised that listening to and performing music brings a great deal of pleasure to many children, and is for some, a rare opportunity to communicate or develop emotion in a constructive way.

However, the report of the Working Group lays salutary emphasis on the importance of appropriate resources. There are three key issues here – staffing, equipment and time. The Working Group recognises that there is a shortage of specialists and that many non-specialist teachers lack training in music and confidence in teaching music. I wholly agree with the Working Group's prioritisation of training, both in-service and on teacher training courses. Secondly, the availability of appropriate equipment is of vital importance, particularly for work with physically disabled students. Here, computers with appropriate peripherals such as touch screen or tracker ball are indispensable.

There are numerous and pressing demands on the curriculum for all pupils. We are in danger of curriculum overload, and this is particularly so in the timetable for pupils with special educational needs where additional inputs may be necessary during the short school day (i.e. speech therapy, physiotherapy, support work from a visiting teacher service). It is important to ensure that music is not displaced from the curriculum for pupils with special educational needs.

## Postscript

Since this article appeared in the December 1991 edition of the *British Journal of Special Education*, the National Curriculum Council published their report to the Secretary of State on the statutory consultation for attainment targets and programmes of study in music (NCC, 1992). While welcoming the Music Working Group's report, the Council rejected the Working Group's conclusion that there should be three Attainment Targets, Performing, Composing and Appraising. Instead, the Council recommended that there should be only two Attainment Targets, combining performing and composing into a single Target, and substituting a new Attainment Target, Knowledge and Understanding, in the place of Appraising. Notwithstanding the virtually unanimous support for the Working Party's conclusions among those who had responded in the course of consultations, there was, it seemed, to be a move away from the practical 'hands on' approach espoused by the Working Party towards a renewed emphasis on theory and knowledge in the teaching of music in schools.

The appearance of the Council's recommendations elicited a vigorous response from musicians and those involved in music education in schools. Simon Rattle, the conductor of the Birmingham Symphony orchestra, led a group of musicians, including many of the most renowned names in contemporary British music, in protesting to the Secretary of State and in publicising concerns that the proposals heralded a return to a passive style of teaching and learning which would concentrate on history and appreciation to the detriment of music-making (Ritchie, 1992). Rattle seemed to encapsulate those concerns in his widely quoted comment that 'theory is the condiment and not the meal'.

At the time of writing, it appears that some of these objections to the recommendations of the National Curriculum Council have been accepted. Kenneth Clarke has stated that the music curriculum will be weighted in favour of the Performing and Composing attainment target and that approximately two-thirds of the time available for music in schools should be spent on this area. It has also been reported that the second Attainment Target has been relabelled 'Listening and Appraising', reflecting at least some of the points made by the Working Group. It seems as if the more flexible and open approach advanced by the Working Group may prevail.

However, there is no change on the fundamental issue of resources. Without proper resourcing, the objectives of the music curriculum – whether in the Working Group's open approach, or in the more traditional format which the National Council appear to prefer – will not be realised. Writing last year on the Working Party proposals, I referred to the universal recognition of the potential value of music education for pupils with special needs and I hoped that adequate resources would be provided to implement those constructive proposals. There has been nothing in the current debate to indicate that further resources would be forthcoming and I do not find grounds for optimism in the present climate. Will we look back and see the Working Party report as mere idealism? – and the National Curriculum counter-proposals as mere irrelevance?

## References

Department of Education and Science and Welsh Office (1991) *National Curriculum Working Group Proposals: Music for Ages 5 to 14*. London: DES/Welsh Office.

Department of Education and Science and Welsh Office (1992) *Music for Ages 5 to 14*. London: HMSO.

McCavera, S, (1990) More Than Music: Music Therapy in the Special School in Baker, D. and Bovair, K. *Making The Special Schools Ordinary? Vol 2*. London: Falmer Press.

Prestage, M. (1991) Article on how handicapped pupils are making musical history. Reported in *The Times Educational Supplement* (4.10.91).

Pugh, A. (1991) Assesses the Music Working Party's Final Report in *The Times Educational Supplement* (27.9.91).

Ritchie, I. (1992) 'Curriculum out of tune with reality', *The Guardian*, (17.2.92).

Swanwick, K. (1986) *A Basis for Music Education*. Berkshire: NFER-Nelson.

Swanwick, K. (1988) *Music, Mind and Education*. London: Routledge & Kegan Paul.

# CHAPTER 10

# Religious Education

*Erica Brown*

## Introduction

During the years that have elapsed since the Education Reform Act 1988, there have often been conflicting views about whether 'special' pupils have different curricular needs from other pupils. There is widespread concern at the present time about the National Curriculum, especially with continuity and progression and pupil assessment. Teachers in special schools share this concern but they also believe that what pupils with special educational needs require more than anything else is to know that they are accepted and that they are given the kind of encouragement in their learning which is an expression of other peoples' faith in them.

The amendments and revisions of ERA 1988 to the Education Act 1944, regarding Religious Education and School Worship, reflect thought and trends in religious education during the last decade. Firstly, ERA refers to religious education rather than religious instruction (the term used in the Education Act 1944). Secondly the Act makes it clear that R.E. should not confine itself to the study of one tradition.

Religious Education is part of the basic curriculum by law although separate from the testing and assessment requirements of the core and foundation subjects of the National Curriculum. In county and controlled schools what is taught must be in accordance with a locally agreed syllabus. Any new local education authority syllabus drawn up after ERA, 1988 must 'reflect the fact that the religious traditions in Great Britain are in the main Christian whilst taking into account the teachings and practices of other principal religions represented in Great Britain'. (ERA Para 2–8(3) confirmed in Circular 3/89 26(1). The Act requires every local education authority to set up a SACRE or Standing Advisory Council for Religious Education, which is composed of four groups, firstly a group which is representative of religious communities in the area while others will consist of representatives from the Church of England (except in Wales), teachers' associations and members from the LEA itself. The function of the SACRE is an advisory one concerning religious education and school worship. The position of Special Schools regarding Religious Education and Worship is covered by The Education Act 1981 and *not* by The Education Reform Act 1988.

Section 12 of The Education Act 1981, reads:

> Provision shall be made to secure that, so far as practicable, every pupil attending a special school will attend religious worship and receive religious education or will be withdrawn from attendance at such worship or from receiving such education, in accordance with the wishes of his parent.

The legislation that Religious Education is not obligatory in special schools, may have pleased those ill informed educationalists who argue that religion belongs to mature adult religious communities and therefore has no place in the lives of children, but there are many teachers who continue to argue that pupils need to have a framework within which they can develop spiritually. At a time when the content and stance of R. E. has been under critical review, I believe that it is right that the spiritual religious development of pupils should not be ignored.

It is easy of course to stereotype special children as those who receive and never give. It is even easier if they have no speech, behave strangely and cannot make decisions for themselves, and it may be hard to acknowledge that we all need to develop self-esteem. We cannot strip away the illusions which society holds, but if we shut out the chances of working through what it is like to be different and if we don't admit that people with disabilities *are* people, we are certainly not offering a balanced curriculum.

It is generally understood that R. E. sets out to teach children about the world around them, giving them a sense of their own identity and of relationships with other individuals and groups. It should also help pupils to convey their feelings and thoughts, to experience and develop an awareness of the spiritual dimension of life and eventually to approach questions of ultimate value. In other words, Religious Education is seen as an ongoing process and the underlying goal is educational and, although the viewpoint of the individual is respected, what is taught does not seek to commend a particular faith or viewpoint.

Most people accept that any curriculum should be integrally related to the nature, experience and needs of those for whom it is devised. And in the context of R. E. this means that what is taught will at first contain little that is formal or explicit; it may even appear to be scarcely 'religious' at all because teachers will be working to lay the foundations without which a mature study of religion is impossible. Indeed, for those children with multiple and profound learning difficulties, R. E. may not be concerned with concepts and skills but will mean tapping depths which are not affected by brain damage or will operate through helping them to express their individuality.

There are numerous occasions during a school day when children bring to us experiences and situations which might be termed as very broadly 'religious'. Therefore it is unusual for R. E. to be confined to one particular period on the special school timetable. Indeed, it is usually integrated into the whole school curriculum, allowing teachers to use situations which arise spontaneously as examples of experiences, values and attitudes which they wish to nurture. Thus the lessons which are taught will extend far beyond the formal curriculum.

Where religious education *is* timetabled it is often taught through topics and themes which are supported by other subject areas. As we have seen, themes do not necessarily have to contain anything explicitly religious for religious education to be taking place, but they will generally give scope for aesthetic, spiritual and creative experience. It is imperative that teachers make detailed plans of the possibilities for R. E. within a theme, taking into account the ability of the children, their background and developing attitudes and skills. The choice of topics should also take into account how far they will nurture the religious understanding and development of the pupils by:

- building on past experience;
- encouraging children to reflect on their own experience;
- fostering positive attitudes to life;
- raising questions about meaning and purpose;
- responding to the present needs of the pupils and providing an essential foundation for exploration at a later stage in their lives;
- assisting the child's own religious quest.

The challenge to the teacher is ensuring that the experiences provided are not only appropriate to the individual abilities of the children but faithful to accepted educational goals for *all* children as well.

Special education, by its very nature, means establishing a broad framework which can encompass the diverse needs of pupils so that they are able to reach realistic and achievable goals from a rich and diverse bank of educational activities. In religious education we aim to give children the paintbox and not the painting – in other words the effective curriculum seeks to give pupils a variety of experiences through which they can develop skills, attitudes and concepts.

### The aims of religious education in special schools

County Agreed syllabuses for Religious Education generally advocate that in the early years of development R. E. aims to help pupils to explore and to understand religion so that later on they will have the skills to accept or reject religion for themselves. But what about the aims of R. E. for pupils with special educational needs? Do the aims remain the same? Can/should we ignore the spiritual development of children? And if we do, are we able to justify abandoning them to experiences without helping them to make sense of them? Or does R. E. which explores questions of meaning and purpose cause even more pain to children who are struggling with disabilities? – I believe that R. E. offers a hope and a promise to special children in a world which often neglects their needs and potential.

In broad terms R. E. in special schools aims to:

- raise questions about meaning and purpose of life;
- develop each child's spirituality;
- awaken a desire to communicate/participate;
- give the opportunity to celebrate all that is best within children's experience and to express joy at their own achievements and those of other people;
- help each child to find an 'inner strength' that will sustain through disappointment, fear, frustration, sorrow;
- live purposefully and positively as individuals and as members of the community;
- foster positive attitudes towards the religious beliefs and practices of others;
- provide teaching which is stimulating and diverse;
- **penetrate the heart of human experience.**

The success of learning will depend largely on the quality of the relationship between the teacher and the pupils. It will recognise an intimate knowledge and understanding of the children: their strengths and weaknesses, different levels of emotional, social and physical maturity and the influence of home and family. Pupils will learn far more from the people who surround them than they will from formal education. Motivation for the child will come from the very positive effect of having someone who wants to listen to (or to watch) what you have to say or how you choose to communicate. Of all things which affect the way in which children learn, the most important yet difficult to describe is the atmosphere that exists in a school, and especially in a classroom, where children are expected to express themselves in a personal way and where their responses and ideas are exposed to the view of others.

## Objectives

Most County Agreed syllabuses for R. E. contain suggested objectives, appropriate to the age and ability of children. Because there is often a great variance between the chronological age and aptitude of 'special' children it is very difficult to suggest appropriate objectives. However the following are based on those most commonly found in Agreed Syllabuses, post 1988, and an attempt has been made to match these to the suggested stages of religious development in Key Stages 1–3. They are perhaps best described as a 'framework' on which the subject or topic content of the curriculum might depend.

By the end of each developmental stage it is hoped that pupils will have been given a range of experiences which will have contributed to:

*Key Stage 1*

- an awareness of self and the wonder of being alive;
- an awareness of physical identity and individuality;
- an experience of feelings such as joy and empathy;
- the development of an interest in the natural world;
- an experience of celebration through active participation.

*Key Stage 2*

- an awareness of self in relation to other people;
- a capacity to form relationships;
- the development of healthy attitudes of self-worth;
- a capacity to acknowledge personal response to emotions;
- a perception of the beauty and the pain of the natural world;
- an experience of celebration through story, festival and ritual.

*Key Stage 3*

- an understanding of self in relation to others and of the interdependence of humankind;
- an understanding that relationships demand response and responsibility;
- an awareness of responsibility for the natural world;
- an understanding of the diversity in ability and lifestyles of other people, learning to value the contribution which each individual makes;
- a capacity to enter sensitively into other people's experience through day to day situations and relationships;
- the development of positive and fairminded attitudes towards a range of religious beliefs and practices;
- an appreciation of the ways in which significant experiences in life are expressed through ritual and celebration.

**Concepts**

The word 'concept' almost defies definition, but in the context of the religious education curriculum, it is understood to mean 'a fundamental idea'. The development of religious concepts will occur not only intellectually but also through emotions, imagination and through experience – it is an 'empathetic awareness' which may be explored at different depths. Therefore the same concept may be explored by pupils at any stage of development but at different levels and in different ways.

The following paragraphs describe some of the concepts that are characteristic at the three stages of religious development outlined and the implications of these for the content of the R. E. curriculum.

*Key Stage 1*

Children need to be helped to an awareness of their own physical capabilities and the need to care for themselves, whilst realising the importance of caring for others. Their sense of corporate responsibility should be widened to the implications of group membership.

Through stories, and sometimes through religious symbols, the first insights into the universality of religion should be introduced. A concept of worship will be developed through joining in festivals, rites of passage, special meals etc.

*Key Stage 2*

At this stage most pupils realise that they have to mix with others. Concepts of love, gratitude and sharing should be reinforced so that children begin to feel empathy with class members and realise that, in some cases, individual success or failure is reflected in the group or vice versa.

Pupils should be starting to understand how they fit into the overall pattern of the natural world and their sense of responsibility towards it should be broadened and deepened. They should also be able to grasp some ideas of how, throughout history, humankind has searched for a meaning to life.

*Key Stage 3*

Understanding the concept of self, suggests that young people will explore their own beliefs and values, abilities and limitations, morality and behaviour. For 'special' pupils this will include elements such as identity, responsibility, loyalty to others, autonomy and 'uniqueness'. Because the relationships of many adolescents may be fraught with difficulties, discussion about interaction between the individual and parents, authority, friends and the opposite sex should all be included in the R. E. curriculum.

As the world of young people continues to expand they become increasingly capable of controlling and exploiting their environment and practical involvement in aspects of conservation will help pupils to understand the importance of caring for their world.

Some, but not all pupils will be able to grasp a concept of 'deity' and for these, a study of the central beliefs of major religions including worship, symbolism and the use of religious language will be valuable.

### Skills

In order that the development of concepts may take place skills need to be acquired. Many of these are common to all areas of the curriculum but there are those which are more appropriately used in religious education. These will include:

- *Communication skills* – such as listening, language (verbal and sign), writing and reading.
- *Investigatory skills* – such as enquiry and discovery.
- *Expressive skills* – such as those found in art, music and drama.

### Key Stage 1

Most children have a natural curiosity and this can be used in such a way that they are helped to discover beauty, order, shape and mystery in the natural world.

At Key Stage 1 of development children will find it very difficult to enter imaginatively into the experiences of other people and they will need help in order to become aware of the needs, desires and intentions of people who do not necessarily conform to the pattern of life with which they are familiar. Most pupils will, however, demand care and concern for themselves but they may need to be brought to a realisation that their peers have similar needs.

An awareness of living life with other people necessitates communication and developing the skill of self expression, either verbally or creatively. Where Makaton or sign language is used, children should be helped to understand that symbols and gesture can be an outward sign of a shared experience.

### Key Stage 2

At this stage pupils will gradually develop the ability to enter imaginatively into the experiences of other people and to appreciate their feelings. Beginning to understand that others base their lives on their own set of concepts and ideals will mean learning that rules and laws exist for the benefit of all. In the previous stage of development, learning to develop self control and self discipline stemmed from a desire to please and to gain approval. At the end of Key Stage 2 pupils should begin to realise that self control and self discipline are an appropriate response to trust. During these years children should become increasingly aware that the care and concern shown to them stems from a commitment and dedication to a code of behaviour which often demands self sacrifice. Therefore, they will need to express their appreciation and to demonstrate that they themselves are capable of showing care and concern for others and the world around.

It is hoped that language will have developed by this stage and that most pupils will be able to express themselves in direct speech. First hand experience of literature is important together with the understanding that, although some stories are not factual, they still have something of value to teach about life.

## Key Stage 3

Whilst young people continue to develop an interest in an ever-widening range of people, they should also be learning to enter into the experience of others at a deeper level in order that they may develop an understanding that others may base their lives on their own concepts and ideas.

Pupils should be encouraged to look in depth at themselves, their personalities and at their actions and the consequences of these for themselves and for others. Children will need to come to terms with their abilities and limitations which exert a powerful influence on their lives. Indeed, by the end of their school career they will need frequent opportunities to consider important issues so that they begin to clarify their own position in society.

Adolescence is often a difficult time for personal relationships, bringing pupils into closer contact with others from many walks of life. They should therefore learn to understand the actions and motives of others, to respect the rights of others and to recognise their own responsibilities. At this stage pupils should be beginning to recognise more fully how language, and facial and bodily expression are used in religion e.g. through festivals and liturgies. Through the use of the expressive arts they will be encouraged to enter into the experiences and emotions of others. An awareness of the language of religious writing used in myth, legend, fable, parable and poem will lead to later religious understanding.

## Attitudes

Since all education is concerned with attitudes, these must be of concern in religious education too. Whilst the R. E. teacher is an educator and should not become an evangelist, there are certain values which it is legitimate to discourage or to seek to nurture.

Schools will need to decide which values they wish to emphasise and then to focus on personal and social development in conjunction with religious education. Determining which attitudes and values a school wishes to promote may be relatively easy. Thinking out how to promote them is among the most important and hardest tasks a school faces.

Essentially there are five kinds of attitudes from which to choose. They are:

## Towards learning

| | | |
|---|---|---|
| *Curiosity* | – | a desire to know more and to understand better. |
| *Ingenuity* | – | 'working things out'. |
| *Integrity* | – | a concern for accuracy in understanding and expression. |
| *Fairmindedness* | – | a respect for the honest belief of others. |

## Towards self

Healthy *self esteem*, which is positive and realistic.

## Towards others

Acceptance and appreciation of others. *Sensitivity* to the needs of others.

## Towards the physical world

*Respect* and reverence for life.

## Towards life

*Responsibility* and *determination* in a quest for meaning, purpose and value.

It is again possible to outline general characteristics at Key Stages 1–3 E. and how these might be developed.

## Key Stage 1

Few pupils in the early stages of development will be ready to accept responsibility, even for themselves. It will be through example, advice and experience that children will come to a realisation that the attitudes and behaviour expected of them are intended to enhance the quality of life.

An understanding of integrity will be very limited and children will have limited experience of the natural world, so a thoughtful attitude towards natural things can only be developed within these limitations. However pupils can begin to show an attitude of responsibility towards their immediate surroundings which will later be extended to the home, environment and school community.

*Key Stage 2*

Children should now be encouraged to establish a personal code of values by which they can live their lives. These will be influenced by their individual understanding of the answers formulated to fundamental questions, such as 'Who am I?' 'Why was I born?' The idea of integrity can be developed so that it permeates into all activities. Children should be encouraged to consider the life-styles of other people, through topic work and by reference to explicit religious education as it arises through their everyday experience. They should gradually become interested in the way in which other people organise themselves and behave, learning that, although others may be different, they are not less valuable as people and are worthy of respect.

*Key Stage 3*

Pupils will need to be encouraged to approach serious issues with an open mind, to look at life in a reflective and enquiring manner and to ask questions about the meaning and purpose of existence.

Young people may need encouragement to value themselves as individuals by developing personal respect and recognising their own abilities and shortcomings. They should, however, be able to consider the personal, moral and intellectual qualities of other people, although they will almost certainly need help in order to appreciate the less obvious values of spirituality, morality and love and to realise that a betrayal of one's values, however secret, is inherently damaging to oneself. In order to enter with imagination and understanding into the religious beliefs and practices of others they will need to develop empathy and sensitivity and a readiness to enquire. As students are encouraged to reflect more deeply on their ever-widening environment they will need opportunities to express positive attitudes of care and concern in practical ways. It is very important that pupils at this stage of development are treated in a considerate manner and that their opinions are listened to.

**Planning the school curriculum**

It is not the function of an agreed syllabus to determine how a school should organise its curriculum. The implementation of the agreed syllabus *is* however the professional responsibility of teachers.

Creating and teaching a school curriculum will inevitably make considerable demands on colleagues. These will include skills of creativity, evaluation, and cooperation, because if we design an R. E. curriculum in special education which is different in character from those used in mainstream schools, it will almost certainly mean excluding pupils from those aspects of religion on which society at large places such value.

The variation in local education authority policy and practice is remarkable. Some LEA's are asking schools to produce a framework of policy for children with special educational needs. Even when this request is not being made, many teachers are eager to plan their own strategies. An approach is therefore suggested which reflects the National Curriculum model of curriculum planning. It also incorporates the concepts, skills and attitudes which are necessary for religious understanding. Three stages of religious development are outlined which roughly correspond to Key Stages 1-3 of the National Curriculum. Although some pupils with special educational needs will function within Key Stage 4 even most able children will find the objectives of Key Stage 3 a challenge.

Curriculum planning will include a number of factors:

(1)  The requirements of the Agreed Syllabus.
(2)  The ability and experience of the pupils.
(3)  The value placed on R. E. in the whole school curriculum.
(4)  The roles, responsibilities and expertise of the staff.
(5)  The way in which learning is organised in the school.

### (1) The requirements of the agreed syllabus.

Most LEA agreed syllabuses list their requirements under three main headings:

- AIMS: the school curriculum should contribute to the fulfilment of the overall aims by laying firm foundations for later understanding.
- OBJECTIVES: these are usually stated in terms of objectives which are seen in terms of concepts/knowledge, attitudes and skills appropriate to the age/ability of the pupils. Many of these concepts, attitudes and skills will be encouraged in other curriculum areas.
- CONTENT: the content section of the syllabus is a description of the areas around which learning should be focused. Careful selection of the content will be necessary according to the experience and understanding of the pupils.

### (2) The ability and experience of the pupils

As with all areas of the curriculum, R. E. must start from the experience of the pupils and their conceptual understanding.

### (3) The value placed on R. E. in the whole school curriculum

The Education Reform Act 1988 stated that the school curriculum should 'promote the spiritual, moral, cultural, mental and physical development of pupils'. Religious education has a vital part to play in the school curriculum if these objectives are to be achieved.

*(4) The roles, responsibilities and expertise of the staff*

It is the responsibility of the headteacher to ensure that Religious Education is valued in the curriculum of the school. This might be best achieved by giving one member of staff the responsibility of coordinating the subject and by writing a policy statement concerning the role of R. E.

A policy statement might include:

- the contribution of religious education to pupils in terms of the school's objectives for the subject.
- the way in which learning is organised and the kinds of teaching approaches adopted.
- the content of the teaching programme and an outline of the topics covered.
- the availability of resources.
- the role of the R. E. co-ordinator.

*(5) The way in wich learning is organised in the school.*

In planning the religious education curriculum the general ways in which learning are organised must be taken into account. For children with special educational needs, the content of the experiences/learning provided will probably relate to the following:

- **Self:** including individuality, growth, feelings and behaviour.
- **Others:** including co-operation, sharing and trust.
- **Natural world and 'the world we make':** including responsibility and creativity.
- **Religion:** including stories, customs, festivals and celebrations, special places, people and religious artefacts.

**Evaluation**

Evaluation of children's achievement is often considered important in providing parents and colleagues with an account of what children are achieving, but recording progress in special schools can be a daunting task. It will often take place as part of the teacher's day to day observance of pupils, noting the questions they ask and observing their actions. The teacher's role is to listen and to prompt in such a way as to encourage children to take further steps in their thinking and their response. I do not believe that we can offer our children the best religious education if we omit to evaluate our own teaching. Self evaluation allows us to look closely at our intentions, to take appropriate classroom decisions, and to make any changes which are necessary. Undoubtedly the best schemes for teacher evaluation are those which individual teachers devise for themselves to suit their own needs and circumstances. However, I strongly believe that asking ourselves some of the following questions is a valuable exercise:

- am I showing concern for each pupil as an individual, encouraging a sensitivity towards others and the forming of relationships?
- does my approach to teaching R. E. fully explore the potential in my classroom, school and the local community?
- does my teaching approach give children ample opportunity to explore their own experience?
- am I giving sufficient opportunity for pupil participation and does my teaching encourage children to ask questions and to express themselves?
- does my teaching provide rich opportunities to develop listening, language and thinking skills? (where appropriate)
- do I show an appreciation of each child's contribution, letting them know that effort is more important than success?
- have the children gained enjoyment from religious education?

It is a sobering fact that a child's view of what happens in the classroom is sometimes quite different from that of the teacher. As a profession we often think that we are providing a learning situation or that what we are saying is clear and easy to grasp. Yet how often do children's reactions reveal that what they have absorbed is something very different from that which was intended?

However we choose to teach religious education in special schools we should set ourselves high standards. In this way neither the content of the curriculum nor the religious development of the children will remain static. It will change and develop.

## References

Brown, E. (1990) 'Signposts and Milestones', *Respect*, Respect Publications, Purley-on-Thames, Berkshire.

Brown, E. (1991) 'Special People in Special Places', *Respect*, Respect Publications, Purley-on-Thames.

DES (1989) *Circular 3/89 – The Education Reform Act 1988 – R. E. and Collective Worship*. London: DES.

HMSO (1988) *The Education Reform Act 1988*. London: HMSO.

Hull, J. (1989) The Act Unpacked, Birmingham Papers in R. E. (1), Derby: CEM.

Musty, E. (1991) *Opening Their Eyes – Worship and R. E. with Children with Special Needs*. London: The National Society.

National Society, The (1990) *Religious Education*. London: The National Society.

# CHAPTER 11

# The Technological Challenge

*Phillip Rodbard*

The impact of 'technology' as a new subject as part of the National Curriculum has undoubtedly met with mixed responses all over the country. Whatever the reaction has been, the outcome has meant considerable upheaval for schools and staff in both ideology and the process of delivery. For children with special educational needs the challenge faced by the schools has resulted in a dramatic increase in the range of experiences and opportunities, but with the emphasis on 'entitlement' the benefits for some have, as many expected, not been as fruitful.

The inclusion of technology as part of the National Curriculum led to what can only be described as 'panic' in many quarters, as many tried to take on board the wealth of implications from equal access and assessment for all children to the new emphasis on design and technological capability with its cross curricular approach. The initial rush of adrenalin by those in the mainstream and the special sector has now hopefully moderated as teachers have come to terms with many of the possibilities and opportunities that have emerged.

Many educators believe that the gradual change over the years from handicraft to craft, design and technology and more recently design and technology had run its course without the added weight of a top down approach to bring all into line. The problem with innovations not at a national level, is that many miss out or just do not want to participate. This was often the case in the special schools where teachers did not have the resources, facilities or inclination to take on board new developments; this led to stagnation for many. Those that wanted to extend their subject had to make considerable efforts not to become out of touch.

Therefore, the National Curriculum for technology has provided the impetus for constructive change within the educational system. The recognition that activities should be broad enough to enable all to participate combined with the variety of routes for achieving design and technological capability, gave all children but especially those with special needs, the opportunity to experience a wider range of activities than the more traditional approaches allowed.

## Problems of assessment

The required mechanism for assessment has enabled a national continuity of progression between the different phases of education and between schools. Such detailed recording of progression has provided the mechanism by which children with special needs will have shown positive achievements (although sometimes in very small steps) in areas not previously considered or examined. Conversely, such in-depth analysis of achievements may, for example, highlight the problems encountered by children with special needs in mainstream schools when compared with their more able counterparts.

Unfortunately, to set up the required detailed recording systems and subsequently to continually monitor the children, all takes an enormous amount of teacher time which cannot but interfere with the work in the classroom.

## Structured guidelines

Technology has been divided into two separate profile components, namely design and technological capability and information technology. Each of these being sub-divided into various programmes of study has provided structured guidelines for teachers. Teachers now have detailed directions on how to provide and extend the range of technological capability for the children. This has been a boon for many teachers, especially those in the special schools where isolation and lack of a cohesive programme of learning has been the main problem. For others the imposed structure appears both rigid and inflexible, and it has been suggested that it could perhaps lead to tunnel vision as teachers focus only upon those areas that need to be recorded.

One of the benefits of focusing on design and technological capability is that these are essentially creative and practical. The traditional approach of learning a large body of knowledge is replaced by the investigation of needs and opportunities, followed by the chance to make or modify something and then to evaluate the solution. This change in emphasis spares those with special educational needs the laborious academic assimilation of facts and gives more opportunities for their creative and practical talents to shine. However, there is still a considerable amount of academic input needed within the process of investigation, design and evaluation. These are areas which children with special needs both in mainstream and special schools find difficult and therefore they need considerable assistance to help them achieve success.

## Changing teaching styles

Another benefit from the change in emphasis from the absorption of facts and skills to working within a design framework is that it has radically altered the style of teaching. The traditional vision of the expert didactically imparting a wealth of knowledge, skills and techniques has, with the introduction of the National Curriculum, changed to that of a partner in the learning process. With the teacher's role altered to that of supporting and providing the avenue for realising individual solutions, it has meant a traumatic change for some, but a welcome transfer for others. Whatever the response, the result in the space of a couple of years is that teachers have become far more involved with the children in the learning process.

The interaction between the teacher and pupil has always been more intense in the field of special needs. The relationships that are formed in such situations should enable an easy change in teaching style to incorporate the range of activities required by the National Curriculum programmes of study. For the special schools in particular, the greatest change in teaching style for the subject specialists has been far more group discussion and less practical work.

The cross curricular nature of technological activities has also prompted much debate and has undoubtedly affected teaching styles. It has probably created more waves within mainstream schools where departments have been much more autonomous than in the smaller special schools. Collaboration with other teachers has been a new experience for many and has prompted much anxiety, although the real problem hindering the separate 'technological' departments jointly working together to deliver the National Curriculum has been in the unsure future surrounding each department. The links with 'technology' suddenly began to appear in areas which previously expressed little interest as subjects strove for status.

The struggle for the future identity of separate subjects is not such a problem within the special schools as specialist teachers, if there are any, would already work much more closely with their colleagues, so it would appear less of a threat. Also, the opportunities for cross curricular work, if it does not already take place, are much easier. Therefore, the real difference for many is that the focus for the thematic approaches is now provided by the programmes of study.

## Forging links

Another positive advantage of the National Curriculum is that it has bought many specialist teachers much closer together. For teachers in the special school where isolation for the individual subject specialists is a common problem, links have been made with colleagues from other schools as they strive to come to terms with all the implications. A common bond has often been formed as local working parties have been set up to provide guidelines and help for all concerned. This is especially true for those teachers whose pupils have severe learning difficulties, where some of their pupils would never reach the attainment targets. Rather than prevent exposure to design and technological capability, the opposite is true, because self-help groups have broken down the programmes of study into much smaller detailed stages whereby pupils are viewed as working towards the attainment targets.

## Equal access: problems and opportunities

The adaptation of the National Curriculum for technology to suit individual special needs has bought a much more cohesive programme for the pupils in the special schools. The recognition that the maximum number of pupils possible should be allowed access, has meant that a much wider range of work is now undertaken, particularly for those pupils with moderate to severe learning difficulties. These pupils will undoubtably find certain aspects more difficult, as indeed will others. The problems involved with designing and evaluating will obviously be felt more by those with learning difficulties whether in mainstream or special schools.

The amount of help children with special needs will need in these areas should not be under-estimated. In mainsteam schools for example, one to one help is often needed by those with special needs if they are to successfully cope with all the problem solving and analytical aspects of the work. In the special schools the smaller pupil/teacher ratio would help somewhat, although problems in these areas would be far greater and may involve a different approach. However, there are always corresponding benefits; the major one being not having to learn a large body of knowledge in the many different subject areas which now come under the technology sphere. The digestion and retention of a great body of knowledge was often a problem for those with special needs while its removal should compensate a little for the more academic elements necessary in working towards design and technological capability.

Problems are often paramount at the investigative stage where those with special needs require extra support or even a compromise of experiences for those with severe learning difficulties. Exploratory work for those with considerable learning difficulties relies very much on the teacher leading the process, with responses to questions being the main means of achieving pupil participation. Subsequent design work is also very limited, involving perhaps some drawing, but mainly the design experience is achieved through a teacher/pupil partnership of ideas and involvement at various levels according to the pupil's ability. The design aspect is, therefore, not quite so applicable for those with more profound and multiple learning difficulties where the responses if achieved, would be automatic and lacking meaning.

When catering for special needs at this level, exposure to the programmes of study is still desirable but the method of achieving the long route to design capability must be very much process led. The 'working towards' element of involvement would be associated very much with tactile experiences and familiar things. However, as the ability level would be around Key Stage 1 or below, it would not necessarily be age appropriate. Therefore, if you take age into account, some elements of the programmes of study, or even a feeling for other levels is required to widen the range of experiences.

The ability to extract certain learning experiences from the programmes of study to suit the individual and collective special needs of a group is now a major consideration for special school teachers, Mainstream teachers may also find that they have to target some areas at the expense of others simply because of the wealth of things to cover.

**Implications of curricular changes**

The changing emphasis from individual projects based upon interest and a limited range of materials, to a system based upon a structured progression of experiences has led to a dramatic change in activities. The traditional separate subject specialist teachers have had to adapt enormously and I believe most have responded to the challenge in a positive way. The use of new materials, technology and processes have provided far greater experiences and it would need a very isolated and preoccupied teacher to ignore the effects of the National Curriculum.

Therefore, it can safely be said that the emergence of national guidelines for the teaching of technology has finally altered the traditional approaches to crafts and the emphasis upon skills acquisition in many of the smaller special schools. However, the change of activities has made many costly facilities redundant or little required as materials and processes have radically altered. In all schools, specialist accommodation is very expensive to change or adapt but it is a particular problem for the smaller special schools as they do not have the monetary resources, or even space, to provide an environment more suited to the type of design and technological activities now necessary.

Many pupils with special needs who were not academically able did respond to the traditional 'making and doing' by acquiring the necessary manipulative skills to successfully make a whole variety of artifacts. The self-esteem gained and the therapeutic benefits from success in practical areas cannot be underestimated. With the emphasis changing from hard resistant materials to a whole range of activities which tend to focus more upon soft materials and processes, then these pupils are now sometimes at a disadvantage compared to those more able. Also, the fine motor skills required by the use of soft materials are often less suited to those with special needs in both mainstream and special schools, where pupils may not have the skills necessary to realize their ideas.

The final result is also of great importance as success in the practical field is much more likely for those with special needs and may be the springboard to achievement elsewhere in the school. Most activities embarked upon now through the National Curriculum will have a successful outcome especially if the teacher acts as a partner in the design process, although the scale and impact of the result will probably be far less in the eyes of the pupils than previous craft projects allowed.

## The importance of INSET

The teacher, if motivated, ought to be able to harness the natural interest of pupils and provide a learning environment wherein new skills can be learnt to enable both success and understanding. But there are many pitfalls and problems hindering the achievement of the positive attitudes and values which are necessary to the balanced progression of these new learning experiences. Especially as many of the activities and materials may be somewhat unfamiliar, this could create considerable difficulties as the teacher may not feel confident in certain areas and could therefore not tackle certain aspects in enough depth or even perhaps, may omit some experiences.

To ensure continuity of progression requires assistance from others: this could be achieved within the school by effective team work or from outside by INSET providers, especially if additional skills are required. Ideally, training from the local authority would be the natural avenue if available, or perhaps from higher education establishments or even from other interested sources such as TVEI.

In-service training is an essential prerequisite to the effective introduction of any change of direction. The initial round of INSET activities obviously focused upon how to incorporate 'technology' as a cross-curricular activity and also, within the separate schools, subjects which came under the technology banner. In particular, much work was focused on developing appropriate methods to utilize the programmes of study, attainment targets and the like. How much time, I wonder, was spent equipping teachers with the skills necessary to carry out the activities confidently and effectively? This is probably more applicable to the special schools, where many subject specialists still focused much of their work on traditional craft or creative activities.

Reluctance to change is a natural occurrence which requires considerable support and guidance to order to overcome fears and anxieties. Therefore, appropriate INSET is required to help change the attitudes and values of the teachers. It is very easy to move the furniture, but to make any changes permanent, considerable in-depth work is necessary from those INSET providers with more of a national perspective.

## Equal opportunities

Another impact of the National Curriculum is that it has provided all pupils regardless of gender the opportunity to participate in technology. Previously, a lot of pre-conceived ideas were imparted either consciously or otherwise which prevented totally equal access. Even in the special schools which pride themselves upon treating everyone as an individual, pupils were often guided by parents, adults and peers in a way which influenced any choices made.

Career aspirations and expectations also played a major part in providing increasingly narrow channels of experience as pupils got older. All these pressures inhibited equal access to traditional subject areas known for their gender associations. Although much progress has been made in overcoming gender stereotyping, much more work was needed. The National Curriculum has helped enormously in removing the channelling effect of choices; some may argue that freedom of choice is paramount and that the now legal requirement of technology is in itself limiting. However, the inclusion of technology as a cross-curricular and discrete subject within schools has enabled much more equal participation.

The use of new soft materials and associated activities would encourage a more widespread willing participation by girls in areas often dominated by boys. This has been seen to have been the case where girls have contributed much enthusiasm and quality to technological work. For students with special needs the chance to participate in more creative and practical activities as a right, can only be good news. However, there is still the limiting effect of some timetabling methods and staffing constraints in many mainstream schools which has led to girls choosing other subjects at examination level.

## The role of information technology

The division of IT into a separate profile component has greatly increased the status of a relatively new subject area. Unfortunately, its separation and cross curricular emphasis has tended to confuse ownership and perhaps participation, especially within each of the discrete subjects which still form the majority of 'technology' teaching in many special schools. In others, where subject specialists may not be available, the cross-curricular implications of IT has meant a major co-ordination exercise to ensure the maximum participation and progression by all pupils. Another problem where no specialist teachers exist, is that class teachers were suddenly launched into programmes of study and assessment, which for many was unknown and daunting territory.

The current dilemma of the smaller schools, special or otherwise, is between either spreading their IT resources very thinly around hoping that all gain equal access, or focusing the resources centrally, and timetabling their use, thereby ensuring adequate participation by all. Problems of this kind illustrate that there is not yet enough provision within the schools to allow most pupils the opportunities to become familiar enough with information technology systems to gain sufficient confidence to support their own learning.

The proper training and updating of staff is essential to build up enough confidence to overcome natural fears and anxieties of anything 'technically complex'; only then will the widespread and purposeful use of IT happen. Each school will need its own 'expert' to provide the necessary support as even minor problems will lead to frustration and IT avoidance. For the small special schools, such a person may not be present, leading to considerable periods of resources laying idle.

Within the mainstream schools IT is used to varying degrees in the many different specialist subject areas, although provision naturally depends upon the vision and enthusiasm of senior staff and individual teachers. However, access to these resources would still be limited because of the size of classes, with those more capable getting increased access, both to stretch them and because they would be more able to work independently.

Schools, teachers and parents have all recognised that the use of IT can enhance learning in many ways and can increase the participation of those pupils with special needs alongside their more able-bodied or mainstream peers. Therefore, IT can be seen more as a tool or stimulus to enable more equal access to other curriculum areas for those with special needs rather than as involving the more in-depth aspects of modelling, control and applications as required by the higher level programmes of study. It does however, provide the opportunity for a wealth of new experiences, and makes learning far more practical which is ideal for those with special needs.

Within the special schools, the benefits of specialist IT use have long been appreciated. The National Curriculum has provided a framework for the more widespread use of information technology than perhaps was either previously considered or undertaken. Even for those with severe learning difficulties, a detailed breakdown of attainment targets in its broadest sense, has been made to offer pupils the opportunity to work towards the different levels as outlined in the statements of attainment.

Therefore, it is widely recognised by those that work with special educational needs, that there is potentially a wealth of opportunities and experiences to be gained by working towards, or to, the attainment targets in information technology. Access for all children in this area is essential provided that certain basic factors are taken into account, such as the individual aims and objectives of each activity, the availability of appropriate resources and suitable stimuli to encourage learning. If all these are planned in detail, in advance, to suit the needs of the individual pupil, then the maximum possible exposure is required not only for IT capability but to stimulate learning in other areas of the curriculum.

## Conclusion

When the National Curriculum was introduced I was extremely fearful that many children would be excluded from the many worthwhile aspects that the new 'technology' as a separate subject had to offer. To the contrary, the introduction of the National Curriculum has provided the initiative for individuals, groups of teachers and other interested parties to get to grips with a new opportunity for changing the direction of design and technological activities for the foreseeable future.

The natural inventiveness of the teacher has overcome my initial reservations as to the problems of tackling the fairly rigid attainment targets and programmes of study. Whilst there was some flexibility, the teachers have increased the participation of those with special needs by breaking down the attainment targets into much smaller steps. The idea of 'working towards' the attainment targets can only be described as 'inspired', and goes to show the dedication and support given to the many rich and varied experiences of 'technology' as outlined in the national curriculum.

Obviously, with such an innovation there were going to be problems, and indeed, problems there were. The rapid introduction caused much confusion and anxiety as traditional territorial boundaries of many subject specialists were laid open to scrutiny. Problems of assessment created many cross curricular headaches for co-ordinators and simply strain for others.

But most of all, teachers were often left floundering through lack of initial support and training. Changes in teaching styles were necessary as teachers had to cope with new investigative approaches using new materials and techniques. The need for a planned programme of INSET for all levels and types of schools was paramount, whereas what emerged was a rushed collection of cross-curricular approaches trying to integrate subject specialists into the new era. Many teachers found themselves out on a limb; many primary school teachers were crying out for help. Special school teachers also had to form links with each other to provide support and direction.

There were obviously some forms of in-service activities organised by local authorities and other interested parties which did provide enormous help for some, and a little necessary guidance for others. Fortunately, there were enough guidelines already within the National Curriculum programmes of study to prevent total panic and enable teachers to amble along until enough help and support was found, often by the initiative of those at the chalk face.

Finally, I believe many teachers have responded positively to the challenge and have led the developments within their own institutions. Those children with special needs in the special schools, I now feel, will have their opportunities and experiences increased dramatically – more so, when they are resourced adequately. For those within the mainstream schools, my real fears are that they will not get the help they require to enable the progress and progression that is their right.

# SECTION 2 –
# CROSS CURRICULA ISSUES

# CHAPTER 12

# Individual v. individualised: into the 1990s

*Caroline Hammond and Geoffrey Read*

'Individual' and 'individualised' are two terms that are in wide usage in relation to the current differentiation debate. But what do we understand by them? What is differentiation? How do 'individual' and 'individualised' relate to it? These are important questions that all teachers need to address.

From the present ambiguous usage of these terms it would appear that there is some confusion over the meaning of them. Some consider them to be interchangable whilst others use them ambiguously; others it would seem have yet to decide! Clarity of usage of any term is essential, particularly when it is such a central interest to those concerned to provide access to the curriculum for children with special needs.

Differentiating the curriculum for individual access is rightly an important topical issue, particularly for those concerned for children with special needs. The place and role of 'individual' and 'individualised' work and experiences in order to provide this access needs to be established. Both of these approaches have a place; however it is important that we understand the differences between them and their functions within the overall curriculum. Understanding the differences is more than a pedantic use of language. 'Individual' and 'individualised' approaches are both strategies for meeting individual needs. However, the way in which they are used and their effect and place within the National Curriculum framework are quite different. Individual work is quite different from individualised work. The former is differentiation by isolating the learning experiences of individual children, the latter is differentiation of a learning experience within the group context, a matching of the individual child and the task within the group context.

**What is 'individual'?**

This is a question that hardly needs to be asked of those in special education as it is an approach that has been widely used over a long period of time. However, perhaps this familiarity has led us to forget what it implies, its background and development over the last two to three decades. Teachers in special education have developed great expertise in devising 'individual' learning programmes to meet the particular needs of their pupils. For a long time 'special' needs in both mainstream and special schools has been synonymous with the use of 'individual' learning programmes. Indeed, many 'statements' have referred to the need for such programmes.

**Individual programmes, why so popular?**

Teachers have found such programmes to be a powerful tool in their work with children, particularly the least able. It offers a mechanism whereby the teacher can focus the child on very small units of learning within particular areas. This allows the teacher to identify learning difficulties in relation to specific skills and has helped them to develop the type of precise diagnostic teaching skills valued within special education. For many less able children it would be difficult for the teacher, pupil and parents to recognise any progression at all within their learning unless it had been broken down into smaller units.

Working towards shorter-term goals has allowed the teacher to quickly identify difficulties when they occur, and subsequently to fine-tune the learning on offer to the child. For the child the use of a 'small steps approach' provides a valuable opportunity for them to experience success in learning. This benefit cannot be undervalued for many children who have low self esteem through limited opportunity to recognise their own success. The close, one to one relationship that can develop between teacher and pupil when using individual programmes provides a further opportunity to build the child's self esteem. For the child who needs specific teaching to develop skills that other children develop in an incidental manner, this form of clearly defined and focused teaching offers a way forward. In addition, some children clearly benefit from the more careful matching of child and task that individual programming offers.

**A cautionary view**

The potential benefits of individual programmes are clear. However we are now at a point in time when, as discriminating professionals, we should reflect on these benefits in the light of more recent evaluation.

Over recent years a number of studies and reports have suggested that the degree of effectiveness of some of these approaches is perhaps not as high as we might perceive. In America the 1960s saw a tremendous growth in the production of programmed learning packages for less able pupils. It was hoped that this form of individual programming would compensate for perceived learning deficits. These techniques were taken up enthusiatically in this country and seen as a way forward by many in special needs. In retrospect the evidence in relation to a number of aspects of these programmes is that they have not fufilled these early expectations. Whereas children may have appeared to make rapid gains over a short period of time it appears that this detriorates over a longer time. Within this country it has been found that intensive skills orientated work has not led to the long term benefits perceived/expected (McConkey, 1981). In addition, the ability of children to transfer skills learnt in isolation for use in a wider context has proved to be disappointing. Teachers of the less able have often found this to be particularly true (DES, 1987, 1991).

It has been suggested that the often decontextualized and narrowly focused nature of some programmes leads to short term gains in skills but at the expense of permanence and the ability to transfer and use the skills in wider contexts. This has been particularly so within the field of reading where there has been a strong interest in isolating component skills and developing specific learning programmes. However, the level of effort and input often does not compare favourably with outcomes. In other words, the teacher spends considerable time constructing and delivering an individual programme and the child puts in considerable effort for what are often only short term gains. It has been suggested that those children that find it difficult to apply skills and learning from one area to another in the curriculum in particular need to develop these within a meaningful learning context (NCC, 1989). Phonic skills learnt in isolation stand out as a particular example of decontextualised learning which less able children find difficult to apply within the wider curriculum (Smith, 1982).

**Background and development of the approach.**

Teachers in special education have shown tireless energy and creativity in seeking ways of presenting an appropriate curriculum and developing their pupils' abilities in steps that are accessible to them. However, in our enthusiasm to make learning accessible some have perhaps overlooked the background to the approaches they use and what is implied by their usage both in terms of how we see our pupils as people and what we believe the nature and structure of learning and knowledge to be. In particular, behavioural approaches have often appeared to be attractive to teachers because of the apparent structure and objectivity that they offer.

Many individual learning programmes have in practice used techniques associated with a behavioural approach that breaks learning down into discrete skills forming 'pyramids' of development. During the 1970s there was a flourishing industry in special schools, and associated literature (for example Ainscow & Tweddle, 1979), producing behaviourally based 'checklists'. At the time these seemed to offer a way forward to those who wished to develop a rationale for the special school curriculum. Unfortunately in the enthusiasm for this development more energy often went into developing the checklist than the supporting curriculum and learning experiences (Swann, 1983). A present day analogy would be an over-emphasis on addressing statements of attainment within the National Curriculum to the detriment of the programmes of study.

Although behaviouralism seems to offer a way forward, the philosophy behind this approach is often overlooked by those using behavioural modification techniques in their practice. One of the strengths of such approaches is that they are often based on empirical research evidence in contrast to much other educational research. However, behavioural approaches are based upon the assumption that 'learning involves change in behaviour' (Merrett & Wheldall, 1987). The focus of behavioural modification is on developing techniques (behavioural schedules) to bring about changes in behaviour. In contrast to other views of education (Hirst, 1970) which see the aims of education as open-ended, those adopting a behavioural view of learning focus upon 'ends' rather than the broader processes of learning.

In the 1970s we fought hard to have all children under the umbrella of education and to be considered educable. Stopping for a moment to consider what this means may help us to clarify the difference between training and education. Hirst (1970) quite clearly draws out a distinction between training, which has a clearly defined product, and education which is said to be an open-ended process more concerned with the overall development of the individual and their mind than with one particular product and set of skills. We can easily confuse the distinction between training and education by over-reliance on behaviouralist methodology. There should be a difference between education and training although there is a place for both within our system. It is important that we distinguish between those occasions when our goals are training or are educational.

Our primary aim is the education of all children and it must be accepted that the broad aims of education are the same for all. Concern for this distinction has been responsible for a growth in the literature about how we view young people with special needs and definitions of being a human being (Aspin, 1982, Burwood and Brady, 1981). Within this literature it is suggested that we adopt implicit and unconscious views of children by the educational techniques that we use. Fagg (1991) cites Billinge (1988) as saying ... 'behavioural objectives models can lead to an unrealistic imbalance with an emphasis on what is being taught rather than on what is being learned: approaches which ultimately degrade the learner, the teacher, and the learning process.' To the practitioner concerned with the everyday nature of teaching children with special needs this may seem divorced from reality. However, sometimes we need to step back from the working situation and reflect on our practice for our own professional development.

## What is 'individualised'?

It would appear that there is more confusion over the meaning of 'individualisation' than 'individual'. An individual programme is one that has been prepared for a single child covering subject matter which is not necessarily being worked upon by other members of the teaching group during that lesson or at any other time. The child following an individual programme usually works in isolation from other members of the group and interaction is minimalised or even frowned upon.

Although individual and individualisation have a number of similar characteristics they are in practice quite different. Both aim to match pupil ability to the learning activity offered. Both seek to present learning in manageable units through which the child and teacher are able to recognise achievement and progression. Both may be valuable tools for the teacher who aims to provide curriculum access for all their pupils. However, the underlying philosophy behind the two approaches is quite different.

Individualisation is not a technique so much as a view of the group and the individual children within it. It is a recognition of the fact that teaching groups are composed of individuals, all of whom have different needs and abilities. It sees the group and group learning experiences as of central value, but wishes to involve and make these meaningful for the individuals within the group. It also recognises the dynamic nature of the group and the individuals' variable abilities in relation to particular activities.

Group learning is a complex and dynamic activity. To see the individual in isolation is to deny the social context and pastoral influences of the group. The teacher can use group experiences to develop skills within individuals and across the group which cannot be offered in isolation. Groups can be competitive and supportive, valuing the individual and the contribution they make. However, if not managed appropriately, a group can also be destructive of the individual and itself, fostering negative experiences and inappropriate learning. The group is a powerful tool which, in the hands of a skilled teacher, offers exciting and challenging learning experiences for children. When managed appropriately it can facilitate access to the curriculum for all children.

## Differentiation within the group

Individualisation of group experiences requires the teacher to have a wider view of the group and individual children within it. Profiling individuals' abilities in relation to specific activities is a central aspect to consider when planning group schemes of work. It must be stressed that this is not the same as setting or streaming a group in some rigid way. The nature of each activity will demand different abilities from pupils which affects potential groupings for the task. A child with poor reading, for example, would need to have a task requiring more advanced reading skills modified in order to make it accessible. However, the same child may have a stronger ability in, for example, mapping skills and may therefore benefit from enrichment of the basic task. The teacher needs to build a broaf profile of each pupil's abilities in relation to the activities they plan to introduce. By building a matrix, cross-referring activities with abilities required, in relation to pupil's, they will be able to more effectively tailor learning experiences to the individual.

Within a teaching scheme the teacher needs to construct goal-focused learning activities which offer meaningful access to all the individuals. These are such that each pupil is able to participate at their own level within one activity ('open' activities); alternatively, the focus of the activity will be modified for individuals, or clusters of individuals, within the overall group. In both instances individuals are engaged in group learning experiences in line with the teacher's aims for the group. The teacher needs to plan for a balance of experiences that both meet the individual needs of pupils and serve the aims that they have set for the overall teaching scheme. Structuring a series of linked activities with, perhaps, lead and follow-up activities also needs to be considered. The individuals' achievements both in terms of group and individual activities must be monitored. Differentiating activities for individuals within the group context undeniably places an additional dimension into the teacher's planning and record keeping.

## Differentiation and the National Curriculum

The Education Reform Act requires us to consider a wide variety of issues and in particular our practice in relation to individual pupils. The National Curriculum includes all pupils, requiring us to reconsider the nature of the curriculum we offer to children with 'special needs'. Although 'differentiation' is a current topical issue which some may see in relation to the National Curriculum, it is not a new concept to the good practitioner. The National Curriculum has brought this to the forefront because of its individualised structure and nature. The National Curriculum has been designed as an entitlement curriculum for the individual. It is an aim of the National Curriculum that each child's progression within the curriculum can be identified on an individual basis. The guidance that accompanies it suggests ways in which we can do this. Differentiating learning activities for individuals through individualisation is one of the strategies which can help us to meet individual needs and allow pupils to progress in accordance with their individual abilities.

The programmes of study have largely been constructed in such a way that knowledge, skills and attitudes have been deliberately intermingled. This picked up the H.M.I. recommendation (DES, 1985) that learning should be a balance between these aspects. Providing a context in which opportunities are offered to explore particular aspects of knowledge, skills and attitudes is now widely seen as an effective rationale for curriculum planning (N.C.C., 1990). The evidence would suggest that decontextualised learning which focuses upon isolated skills or aspects of knowledge is not effective in the long term. Children tend not to blend learning achieved in this way into a broader use and application in different situations that they might encounter. It tends not to build towards the type of objective, independent and critical view of the world valued in a more traditional (rationalist) approach to education (Blenkin and Kelly, 1987, O'Hear, 1987).

The rationalist view of education stresses the development of an 'educated' mind through a curriculum centred upon forms of knowledge (Hirst, 1965). This form of education is seen as structuring and developing the mind in such a way as to promote an independent, appreciative but critical view of phenomena within the world. Through the forms of knowledge a person is said to be able to develop 'universal' and logical theories which have wide application. For example, the study of Latin is seen as mind-forming and promoting the development of logical thinking which would have wider usage and application. Although this approach to education may be valid for some it can exclude many pupils.

It would appear that the writers of most of the National Curriculum programmes of study have sought to find a balance between the type of education which promotes the 'mind-forming' and that fosters the ability to apply learning across contexts alongside one that acknowledges the central importance of context-based learning. The 'using and applying' attainment targets are examples of the importance placed on process and application of learning. The importance of problem solving and deductive learning which encourages theory-building and rule-forming based upon experience are promoted throughout the programmes of study, non-statutory guides and 'Curriculum Guidance' series. Providing a context in which broader learning can occur is therefore at the centre of the National Curriculum. This context-based learning is consequently an entitlement for all children.

Individualising work within the group context is a way of offering this entitlement and is also consistent with the aims of the National Curriculum. The National Curriculum has been constructed largely as a spiral curriculum which allows for individual pupils within the group to develop knowledge, skills and attitudes at different levels. Teachers are able to construct learning activities in such a way that individual pupils can access them an their appropriate level of working. This is possible without the need for some pupils to be working on different areas of learning to those of their peers. Individualising tasks is therefore not only facilitated by the structure and organisation of the National Curriculum but is also advocated within the supporting literature (N.C.C., 1989) as well as offering an effective method of meeting individual needs.

The National Curriculum is a 'curriculum for all'. Although there are some undeniable problems associated with it, it has offered those in special education a way forward in developing the curriculum for children with special needs. It has 'normalised' the curriculum and encouraged us to view all children within the same framework. Through the Education Act 1981 many LEAs have sought to integrate those with special needs into a common educational system. In many cases this has been seen as more than merely placing children within mainstream schools. Some have seen this as an opportunity to bring about 'comprehensive' education in its true sense (Hegarty, 1982). The National Curriculum has further fostered an egalitarian view of education and is implicitly pro-integrationalist in the widest sense. We must therefore not undermine this by retaining teaching practices which widen the gulf between 'normal' children and those with 'special needs'.

Individual learning programmes are not necessarily antithetical with the aims and structure of the National Curriculum. There is a place for use of this technique within the range of ways that learning may be offered. However, such programmes must clearly be used judiciously if we are to keep faith with broader educational goals and the wider ideals behind the National Curriculum. They are not always effective ways of offering learning because of their de-contextualising nature. They accentuate differences between so called 'normal' children and those with 'special needs' and the strategies each respective group's teachers employ (Swann, 1987); this can ultimately be 'anti-integrationalist'. Teachers must also consider the moral question of whether it is appropriate to use techniques in individual programmes which do not implicitly promote independence and autonomy in its widest sense. Finally, they do not sit easily within the structure of the National Curriculum and its guidance and do not promote the group learning experience.

## Into the 1990s

What of the future, and how do we use the ideas of individual and individualised in the practical classroom situation to make learning and our teaching more effective? Individualising, or differentiating for the individual, is not a new concept and has always been a feature of effective teaching.

> Between the brightest and the liveliest on the one hand and the dullest and the most reserved on the other the range of intelligence and the degree of social

adaptability are usually too great to justify any teacher on relying solely upon class instruction as a method of education. (Handbook of Suggestions for Teachers, 1937, Board of Education)

This book of suggestions goes on to further point out that

> The child learns in many ways, sometimes best as a member of a large group, sometimes best as a member of a small group, sometimes best individually . . . The teacher must . . . know how to adapt his instruction to the several needs and capacities of his pupils.

This basic guidance remains as pertinent for us today as during the inter-war period. Within the context of the National Curriculum we must find ways of offering learning in a variety of ways to our pupils which take into account their differences in all respects. Difference is to be celebrated not disparaged. As was recognised in the above-mentioned handbook, children may need learning to be presented in a variety of ways, including on an individual basis.

Several strategies have been mentioned to help the teacher to become more fully aware of the range of differences within and between their pupils. The central role of the group and its power as a learning environment has been discussed. However, the teacher also needs to see the group as a constantly dynamic group of individuals. Clustering individuals and modifying activities should not be seen as fixed in relation to individuals. Teachers need to consider the group afresh for each activity that they have planned in order to avoid the well known problems associated with streaming, and consequent labelling. Children need to see that groupings within the class are focused upon particular activities and not on their perceived generalised 'ability'.

Gaining a more detailed and intimate knowledge of individuals and the group as a whole is the key to providing access. One way in which the teacher can do this is by 'profiling' an individual's range of abilities and skills. It is important that this is done across a wide range of curriculum areas and is not, as is often done, restricted to particular skill areas such as reading. Skills in PE, music and art also have an important cross-curricular role in profiling. Armed with this type of broadly based profile of information the teacher is in a better position to more accurately match learning to pupil needs and abilities. They should also be able to more clearly identify the social interaction and learning which is an important part of a child's education.

Many teachers find that they are able to provide a greater degree of access for their group as a whole by structuring their teaching programmes into a series of whole group (led) activities and small group/individual (follow-up) activities. The teacher is able to present new ideas within a learning area to the whole group through a led activity which is designed to provide access for all members of the group. Subsequent follow-up activities which develop this learning can then be offered to smaller groups and, where necessary, individuals. This allows the teacher to enrich the learning experiences for some and to reinforce or develop those of others. When the teacher wishes to move the group on they are then able to offer another lead activity which builds upon earlier learning. Subsequent follow-up activities are then planned, and so on. This model allows the teacher to offer group learning experiences whilst differentiating between the needs of individual members. They are able to build upon shared learning which includes all children in an appropriate way. When planned appropriately all members of the group are offered learning experiences which are not only accessible but also 'stretch' them and provide opportunities for their development. In our desire to provide access we must make sure that we still offer rigour and challenging learning experiences in a meaningful way. Meaningful access is not merely offering learning at the lowest common denominator of ability.

Effective teachers have always placed great emphasis on planning learning experiences for their pupils. Careful planning is crucial to the enterprise of providing meaningful access for individuals within the National Curriculum. The National Curriculum also requires us to plan in order to forecast teacher assessment opportunities. Covering the programmes of study within the context of the 'whole curriculum' places great demands on planning both at the class and whole-school level.

In conclusion, we have tried to draw out the ambiguities over the terms 'individual' and 'individualised' that seem to be occurring at the present time. We have placed this within the context of how we teach and the beliefs we carry. Individualisation, or as it is more widely known, differentiation, is an effective teaching practice that is neither new nor uniquely part of the National Curriculum. It is a practice that is the hallmark of a good teacher regardless of the ability of their pupils. Like most effective teaching skills it is not accidental. It requires preparation and forethought in our teaching at all levels of curriculum planning. An essential component of meaningful differentiation and access is a dynamic view of the group and a positive and flexible view of individual children's abilities.

## References

Ainscow, M. and Tweddle, D. A. (1979) *Preventing Classroom Failure: An Objectives Approach*. Chichester: John Wiley.

Aspin, D. N. (1982) 'Towards a concept of human being as a basis for a philosophy of special education', *Educational Review*, 34, 2, 113–123.

Blenken, G. M. and Kelly, A. V. (1987) *The Primary Curriculum*. London: Harper Educational.

Burwood, L. R. and Brady, C. A. (1981) 'Philosophical Models of Man: with special reference to the teaching of ESN children', in *Educational Review*, 33, 1, 17–23.

Department of Education and Science (1985) *The Curriculum from 5–16: Curriculum Matters 2, an H.M.I. series* (H.M.S.O.)

Department of Education and Science (1987) *Better Maths, A Curriculum Development Study – low attainers in mathematics project*. London: H.M.S.O.

Department of Education and Science (1991) *Differentiation in Action*. London: H.M.S.O.

Fagg, S. (1991) 'Perspectives on The National Curriculum', in: Ashdown, R., Carpenter, B. and Bovair, K. (eds) (1991) *The Curriculum Challenge*. London: Falmer Press.

Hegarty, S. (1982) Integration and the 'Comprehensive' School, *Educational Review* 34, 2, 99–105.

Hirst, P.H. (1965) 'Liberal Education and the Nature of Knowledge', in Archambault, R.D. (ed) *Philosophical Analysis and Education*. London: Routledge and Kegan Paul.

Hirst, P.H. and Peters, R.S. (1970) *The Logic of Education*. London: Routledge and Kegan Paul.

McConkey, R. (1981) 'Education without understanding', *Special Education Forward Trends* 8, 3, 8–10.

National Curriculum Council (1989) *A Curriculum for All*. Curriculum Guidance 2. York: NCC.

National Curriculum Council (1990) *The Whole Curriculum*. Curriculum Guidance 3. York: NCC.

O'Hear, A. (1987) 'The Importance of Traditional Learning', *British Journal of Educational Studies* 35, 2.

Smith, F. (1982) *Understanding Reading: A Psycholinguistic Analysis of reading and learning to read*. New York: Holt, Rinehart & Winston.

Swann, W. (1983) 'Curriculum Principles for Integration', in Booth, T. and Potts, P. (eds) *Integrating Special Education*. London: Blackwell.

# CHAPTER 13

# Topics: from Myths to Objectives

*Richard Byers*

## What is a topic?

''Ere, Miss, what's this?' A dead butterfly is offered up to teacher's attention on a small palm.

There is a pause in the babble of the mixed ability class of nine-year-olds. It is as if the children, like the teacher, sense the pivotal nature of this moment.

'Ah, Shane', says the teacher, 'that is interesting. Do you think you and your friends could find out what it is and tell me something about it?'

Seizing the moment, the teacher is aware that this spark of interest, the product of childish curiosity, might become a useful topic for the whole class. She adds tinder to the spark by directing the children to some new books in the school reference library. She fans the flame with some posters and wallcharts borrowed from the professional development centre and soon the idea is ablaze.

Some children make butterfly paintings. Others embroider butterfly patterns onto pieces of hessian. All the children have a go on the computer, generating wing designs and discussing symmetry. One group of studious children produces meticulous graphs demonstrating the decline in population of rare butterfly species. A parent who is an amateur lepidopterist hears about the topic and helps the children to set up a vivarium in the corner of the classroom. A breeding colony of huge tropical swallowtails is established and all the children are able to observe and record the details of a butterfly's life cycle.

Soon the children have filled colourful project folders with fascinating data. They have created stunning wall displays based on their research and art work. They suggest that they would like to put on an assembly for the whole school, so that they can show off all the work they have done. Two weeks later, before an entranced audience of pupils, teachers and invited governors, they put on a delightful show. They read out the butterfly haikus they have written, summarising the ephemeral quality of existence, and they perform the dance they have devised to symbolise the metamorphosis of caterpillar to butterfly. The assembly serves as a fitting end to a term in which one dead butterfly has inspired a rich extravaganza of cross-curricular learning experiences.

## The prevailing myth

This example illustrates the classic topic myth – an educational device whereby the natural curiosity of young pupils can be harnessed and channelled by an imaginative and responsive teacher in order to produce a vehicle for learning by discovery. Many of the essential elements of the topic, theme or project approach are displayed. The work is pupil-led, inter-active and collaborative. It involves problem-solving and creative inquiry across subject boundaries. The tasks for different pupils are open-ended and relevant to their own needs and interests, allowing the teacher to function more as a guide or director than as an instructor.

This is an engaging model for educating young pupils and, of course, topics can be seen to be working in this sort of way in primary and middle schools around the country. But what would have happened to that butterfly had Shane brought it into a school for pupils with severe learning difficulties? Cynics might suggest that it would have been eaten by one of the pupils and that would have been the extent of the curiosity displayed.

Yet topic is currently a buzz word in schools for pupils with severe learning difficulties. Around the country, the topic is seen as the answer to many of the problems presented by the National Curriculum to teachers of pupils with severe learning difficulties. Visitors to schools for pupils with severe learning difficulties are commonly shown big wall displays in the school hall labelled 'Our Community' or 'The Weather' and told: 'Here is our topic for this term'.

So what, in reality, is the nature of the topic methodology? Where does it come from? Why are special schools so interested in it just now? And is it truly relevant to the needs of pupils with severe learning difficulties? This chapter sets out to examine some of the issues raised by these questions and to indicate the possibility of a way forward.

## The development of the topic approach

The 'topic approach' is a convenient catch-all term which represents a set of ideas which have existed under a wide variety of banners over many years. Yendoll (1988) traces the history of the topic back to William Cobbett in England in the early 19th century and through a succession of American

148

educationalists, Kilpatrick, Parkhurst and Dewey among them, in the early part of the 20th century. But it was with the 1960s that the topic approach came of age in Britain. The Nuffield Foundation and the Schools Council were committed then to a kind of education which offered pupils the freedom to make discoveries in their learning – to gain concepts through exploration and experience rather than learning drills and formulae by repetition.

In 1967 the Plowden Report on primary education lent its weight to the idea of teaching by topics and it seemed that teachers had adopted the method with enthusiasm. Teachers and educationalists saw the topic approach as having a number of powerful advantages. Kent (1968), for instance, felt that topics encouraged pupils to be active participants in their own learning and to use their initiative. He believed that topics made learning relevant to the world beyond school, motivated pupils to acquire basic skills, promoted collaborative group learning and problem solving, and gave pupils some sense of control over their own learning environments. He saw topics as opportunities to take advantage of pupils' spontaneous enthusiasms and to blur the boundaries between subjects. Furthermore, he stated that young pupils liked topics because they were able to pursue their own interests and to indulge their 'inherent curiosity'.

By the late 1970s, however, the topic approach was being subjected to severe criticism from all sides and not least by Her Majesty's Inspectorate (DES, 1978). It seemed that the topic approach had gone badly wrong and that primary education was in danger of becoming superficial, random and fragmented. Teachers were criticised for not planning work properly and for indulging in unnecessary repetition so that basic skills and essential ideas were not being taught. Writing in the *Times Educational Supplement*, Eggleston (1980) and Thomas (1982) continued the critical onslaught. It seemed that teachers were failing to set objectives in their teaching. Pupils' individual needs were not being assessed or catered for and their full potential was not being challenged or realised. Progression and continuity were seen to be suffering because of poor, or non-existent, record keeping and evaluation. Pupils, Eggleston claimed, were being subjected to an endless series of ill planned topics without learning or achieving very much of any real educational consequence.

Clearly teachers in special schools would be advised to avoid adopting any methodology which could lead to such aimless, superficial teaching in practice. Yet the topic approach has survived the criticism and teachers are again addressing cross-curricular issues through the use of topics. The National Curriculum itself acknowledges the importance of cross-curricular approaches, both via the cross-curricular elements, the dimensions, themes and skills, and through the deliberate links and overlap between subjects. Further it is plain, looking at the programmes of study and the attainment targets for the core and other foundation subjects, that a peer-supported, collaborative, experiential, problem-solving approach is often actively required of pupils working within Key Stage 1. The work is often process-orientated – concerned with 'how' children learn as well as with 'what' – as is exemplified in the statutory orders for technology, for instance (c.f. Smith, 1991).

This must present teachers in schools for pupils with severe learning difficulties with a challenge. Traditionally their approach has been founded upon the setting of tight, precise objectives and upon the teaching of clearly defined individual skills, often one-to-one, with the rigorous assessment of progress informing the setting of further objectives. The work, in other words, is product-orientated – concerned with the new skills that children acquire and that can be observed and measured against various pre-arranged criteria. Indeed, special school teachers have, of late, sometimes taken to criticising themselves for being too prescriptive, too directive and too closed in their approach. It is possible that the very rigour which is applied to objectives-based teaching in schools for pupils with severe learning difficulties can cause skills to be taught out of context and pupils to become adult-dependent. Furthermore, choosing a variety of unrelated individual targets for each pupil from an array of subject-specific programmes does not always provide a coherent scheme of work for that pupil.

The topic approach and the tradition of objectives-based teaching stand in contrast to one another. Both methodologies have their strengths and their disadvantages. The challenge facing teachers in special schools is to try to reconcile the two approaches, capitalising upon their advantages while avoiding the pitfalls of both (c.f. Ashdown, Carpenter and Bovair, 1991).

## Integrated schemes of work: a synthesis

It would seem, in theory, that the topic approach and the objectives-based teaching approach complement one another rather neatly. The topic approach has, as I have indicated, been criticised in the past for failing to offer progression, a range of activities and contexts appropriate to varying learning needs or the teaching of basic skills. Critics have identified a lack of continuity and of adequate planning, assessment, evaluation and record keeping. However, all of these elements are essential features of the objectives-based approach – the traditional mainstays of teaching in schools for pupils with severe learning difficulties are precisely planning, assessment, record keeping and the teaching of basic skills through programmes of objectives tailored to individual needs.

Conversely, the objectives-based tradition is now criticising itself for being too closed, prescriptive and adult-led, with tasks being set for pupils out of context. The topic approach, on the other hand, actively encourages pupils to choose how and what they learn, through problem-solving, discovery and working with others in open-ended activities which they can relate to their own experience.

The idea of a synthesis between the two approaches ought, therefore, to be an exciting possibility, offering teachers in schools for pupils with severe learning difficulties the opportunity to have the best of both worlds. The potential for broadening the scope of the special school curriculum to encompass the requirements of the National Curriculum without threatening to undermine the solid foundations of traditional special school methodology is apparent. If such a synthesis looks attractive in theory, how will it work in practice?

The National Curriculum Development Team (SLD), based at the Cambridge Institute of Education, devoted a major part of the school year 1990 to 1991 to trialling National Curriculum work in schools for pupils with severe learning difficulties in the local education authorities of the DES Eastern Region. Much of this work involved planning and recording work in cross-curricular contexts. The team suggested that teachers develop their ideas beyond the initial stage of the topic web. Topic planning appeared to progress most effectively when teams of teachers were involved. Working groups rapidly generated ideas for a variety of topic related activities. Indeed, topic webs were often seen to grow alarmingly quickly in a diversity of directions, suggesting that a reflective, tightly-focused editing phase might improve topic webbing immensely. Once a satisfactory range of ideas for topic related activities had been agreed (ideas which hopefully arose out of genuine practice rather than out of any idea of what a topic 'ought' to look like), planned activities were referenced to the National Curriculum programmes of study and to the schools' own curriculum documents.

From this curriculum-referenced bank of activities, teachers were able to devise what the team called 'integrated schemes of work' for their class group or for individual children. These integrated schemes of work comprised clusters of objectives related to the topic theme. In terms of teaching and learning styles, it became apparent that some of these objectives would be familiar behavioural targets of the 'by half term, Jenny will, under these circumstances . . .' variety. Others would represent more open-ended 'learning encounters' whereby individual pupils or groups of pupils would have opportunities to make discoveries, or solve problems. The idea was that programmes of objectives would consist not of separate paths through different subject areas; nor of creative but chaotically unplanned experiences; but would be shaped into a coherent matrix of linked targets which could be approached within a controlled cross-curricular context (see Figure 1).

## Integrated schemes of work in practice

An example may help. Suppose that the whole-school topic for next term is

**Figure 1**

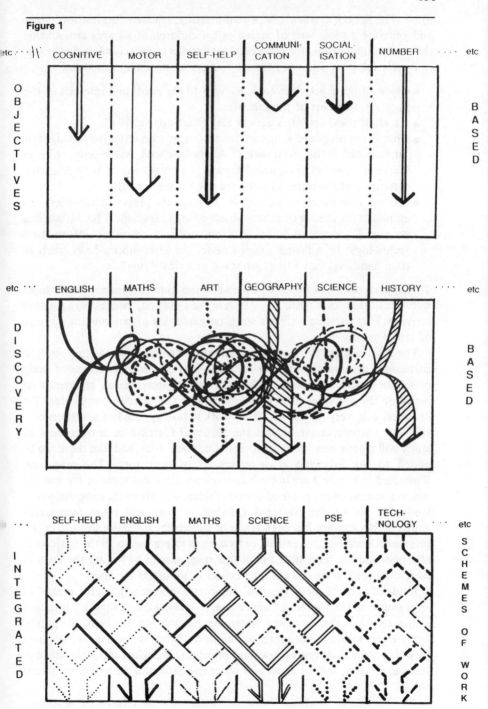

to be 'The School Garden'. At a staff meeting, teachers 'brainstorm' ideas and generate a topic web of activities for children of all ages around this theme. Planning teams for different departments in the school then take this raw material away and ask themselves a set of searching questions:

- which of these activities look relevant to the needs and interests of the pupils in this part of the school?
- are all of these activities age- or Key Stage-appropriate?
- what is the proposed structure for this topic – an intensive fortnight of 'immersion' in the given theme? A whole school, whole term, 'fit it in where you can' extravaganza? Or a half a term's worth of 'Wednesday afternoon Humanities sessions for the Lower School'?
- is there a common thread running through the proposed activities – an emphasis on science or other subject-related experiences for instance; a core skill focus such as problem solving or using information technology; or a theme which stresses the inter-subject links, such as data handling, or sorting, grouping and classifying?

This sort of selection process can lead to the kind of slimmed down topic web illustrated in Figure 2 – a few well-defined, accurately-targetted activities summarising a term's work on gardening afternoons for a group of senior pupils.

The next task for the staff is to relate the activities from the topic web to curriculum documents, whether National Curriculum programmes of study or school programmes and checklists. It will be immediately apparent that many of the activities are cross-curricular – the 'garden diary' idea, for instance, will, very obviously, entail work in history, English and science. It will also become apparent that the National Curriculum programmes of study will inspire new ideas for topic-related activities, and that these can be added to the lists and cross-referenced in their turn. The references illustrated in Figure 3 are not exhaustive, but represent some of the ways in which a sample of the planned activities relate directly to the programmes of study for six of the National Curriculum core and other foundation subjects. No attempt has been made to stretch these relationships to create references which are tokenistic, or to drag in references to all the subjects at all opportunities. The intention at this stage should be to find the ways in which the topic plan and the curriculum fit naturally together.

Evidently the 'School Garden' topic is a potentially useful means of engaging with the National Curriculum. It is also evident that this is to be a well-planned topic, enabling extensive records to be kept of pupils' experiences within the programmes of study. What is not clear is the extent to which individual pupils' learning priorities, including those identified at Annual Review, will be addressed when the gardening activities begin next week.

At this stage, working from the collection of referenced activities,

**Figure 2**

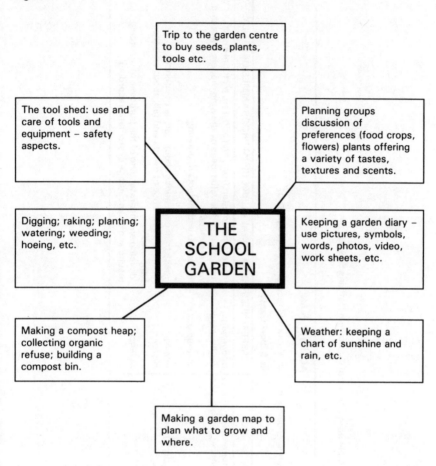

individual teachers, or small groups of teachers working in team teaching or unit situations, can plan integrated schemes of work for groups of pupils or for individuals. This will mean developing well differentiated, age-appropriate, detailed schemes of work from the activities identified on the topic web; 'task analysing' those activities to create well defined mini-activities for specific children; and weaving ongoing, high-priority objectives through the topic-related activities. The process will produce programmes of realistic activities, summarised in precise objectives, which:

- have continuity with previous programmes;
- ensure progression into new, or more refined, skills;
- distinguish between the needs of different children;
- retain the relevance and coherence of the topic context.

154

**Figure 3** Integrated Schemes of Work (a sample from a National Curriculum Planning Sheet)

**ACTIVITY PLAN:**

Planning; planting; maintaining and recording the progress of

**The School Garden:**

| LEARNING STRATEGIES: | REFERENCES TO NATIONAL CURRICULUM PROGRAMMES OF STUDY: |
|---|---|
| Making a 'Garden Map' from a collage of materials; planning what to grow; 'what shall we plant beside the potatoes?' etc. | *Geography:* – 'extract information from, and add it to, pictorial maps'<br>*Technology:* – 'represent and develop ideas by drawing models...working with materials'<br>*Mathematics:* – 'recording with objects or drawing'. |
| Keeping a 'Garden Diary' or 'Garden Calendar' using photos, words, pictures, charts, video, etc. | *English:* – 'make their own books about...areas of interest'<br>*History:* – 'identify a sequence of events and talk about why they happened'<br>*Science:* – 'develop an understanding of the purposes of recording results and so encourage systematic recording' |

**Figure 4**  Integrated scheme of work
*'The school garden'*
*Class 2: Week One*

| | |
|---|---|
| *Mary:* | will change from trainers to wellington boots unaided on request (Self help) |
| *Carl:* | will distribute pairs of gardening gloves to the class on request (Maths; PSE) |
| *Jenny:* | will push and pull the rake from her wheelchair (Science; Physio; Gross Motor) |
| *Tim, Liz and John:* | will negotiate a 'shopping list' of seeds they want to buy (English; Technology) |
| *Fatima and Paul:* | will plant a row of seed potatoes 'this far' apart using a measuring stick and a dibber (English; Maths, Technology) |
| *Jenny, John and Carl:* | will start a 'Garden Map' using pictures cut out of catalogues and collage materials (Geography; Maths; Science; Technology) |
| *Mary, Tim and Fatima:* | will start a 'Garden Diary' – "today we planted lettuce seeds" etc – using words, pictures and video (History; English; Science) |
| *Whole Group:* | will wash and dry their hands after gardening sessions – prompts as necessary (PSE; Self Help) |

The integrated scheme of work illustrated in Figure 4 is intended as a fictitious sample of objectives set for an imaginary group of pupils. It is worth noting that some of the examples give a 'real life' context to traditional objectives of the self-help type, while others deliberately set up situations where group inter-dependency and collaborative problem solving will be required of the pupils. It is also worth noting that a range of basic skills in different subjects will be addressed in a cross-curricular fashion.

## Structures and strategies

Although the topic illustrated in this chapter is a traditional whole school, whole term event, the integrated schemes of work model is intended to be a flexible one. It would be possible for instance, to plan a whole school assembly as a 40-minute integrated scheme of work around a central theme. Individual teachers may wish to plan a whole day's activities around a theme once a week; some will wish to have topic time as a regular slot on their class timetable; others may prefer to work in an integrated way all the time. And, of course, there will continue to be a place for the traditional whole school topic generating wall display material that is supportive to pupil learning over a longer time. The intention is that the format of integrated schemes of work might help schools for pupils with severe learning difficulties to see how they can teach in a cross-curricular way without losing educational rigour.

Integrated schemes of work represent an attempt to combine the virtues of the topic approach with the virtues of the objectives-based tradition in the belief that these virtues are complementary. The assumption behind integrated schemes of work is that bringing together the two approaches will minimise the shortcomings of each while enhancing the educational merits of both.

Many issues remain to be resolved in practice. There is, for instance, the contrast between setting objectives for individual pupils and planning more open-ended learning opportunities for groups of pupils. Eisner (1969) described a process of setting 'expressive objectives' which do not define the outcome of an educational experience. Instead, they identify the nature of that experience by means of strategies designed to promote exploration and discovery. Eisner's terminology is, perhaps, not useful, but the concept is one which teachers of pupils with severe learning difficulties will have to explore if they are to deliver the National Curriculum in the right spirit.

Many schools for pupils with severe learning difficulties have tended to base their practice upon one-to-one teaching styles involving 'precision teaching' and 'errorless learning'. If the National Curriculum suggests a reappraisal of the exclusive use of these approaches in order to provide pupils with problem-solving and discovery-making opportunities, it also requires, in many instances, that pupils work in group situations which emphasise the social nature of the learning process. Rose (1991) describes a range of techniques, for example jig-sawing a task, which facilitate meaningful group activity in classrooms and in schools for pupils with severe learning difficulties. Teachers will also need to take account of these ideas in their planning.

The National Curriculum Development Team (SLD) encouraged planning in terms of 'teaching strategies' referenced to the National Curriculum programmes of study. Teaching strategies do not necessarily specify the end results of pupil activity in the way that traditional objectives tend to do. Further, they take account of planned opportunities for group work. The examples in Figure 4 may serve to illustrate the issues. Mary's objective is a straightforward behavioural target relating to her self help programme. The only novel aspect is that Mary will be learning to change her shoes in the context of a 'real life' situation.

Carl also has some specified behaviour to perform, but there are other levels implied in his objective. Certainly Carl will be distributing gardening gloves to his peers on a one-to-one correspondence basis (maths), but he may also choose to engage in social interaction as he does so. For Carl, who is a socially isolated figure, eye contact or a smile would be significant in terms of his personal and social development. This sort of outcome could not be specified in terms of 'success or failure' criteria, but an opportunity, an encounter, is planned and will be provided.

Similarly Fatima and Paul have, on one level, been given a simple, practical task to perform. They will use a dibber and a measuring stick (use of simple hand tools and use of a non-standard measure) to plant the potatoes. However they will not be directed or closely supervised in this task. They will be left with individual roles to negotiate within the activity (English: listening and giving weight to others' opinions. technology: realise that, when working in teams, people may have specialist roles) and the problem of how to use the tools to solve collaboratively.

Encouraging exploration and investigation through group endeavour means planning the 'how' of teaching as well as the 'what'. It also entails flexibility in record keeping. A system which records success or failure in a defined task with a predetermined outcome will not take account of a variety of pupil responses to a variety of situations. There will, inevitably, be a variety of unforeseen, and perhaps surprising, responses to opportunities which have a truly 'exploratory' or 'investigative' character. An approach is required which permits a focus upon educational process as well as upon product, not in opposition to or instead of the objectives-based tradition, but in order to complement and enrich that approach.

This complementary relationship between process and product is reflected in the form of the National Curriculum. The National Curriculum Development Team (SLD) used the programmes of study, rather than the attainment targets in schools, in order to plan work and record pupil progress day by day, week by week. Achievement in relation to statements of attainment will, of course, need to be recorded when it occurs but, for many pupils with severe learning difficulties, attainment targets will prove to be extremely distant objectives. The attainment targets will ultimately enable teachers to assess and report upon pupil achievement. They constitute the goals which teachers and pupils will need to hold in view.

The programmes of study, however, are descriptions of the means whereby those goals may be attained. They demonstrate the relevance of the National Curriculum to current good practice in schools for pupils with severe learning difficulties and offer ideas for extending work in the various subject areas. The integrated schemes of work approach capitalises upon the cross-curricular potential of the programmes of study for Key Stage 1.

## Conclusion

By the end of the project, the National Curriculum Development Team (SLD) was aware that integrated schemes of work, together with other refinements of the topic approach pioneered within individual schools and LEAs, were being seen as one useful way of delivering the National Curriculum in schools for pupils with severe learning difficulties throughout the country.

There is no fast fix solution, however. The practical problem of recording group experiences and individual responses, without generating vast files of paperwork, exercises many schools still. So also does the question of chronological age versus Key Stage. Topics do enable teachers to offer age appropriate experiences to their pupils, and often these may be relevant activities suggested by the programmes of study for Key Stages 2, 3, or 4. However, Key Stage 4 experience may lead to attainment which barely reaches level one, if it is honestly measurable in terms of statements of attainment at all. Given careful planning this does not have to be a problem. Many schools are differentiating activities from the later Key Stages in order to facilitate level one achievement within the context of the age appropriate activities to which older pupils are entitled. At the same time it is possible to interpret Key Stage 1 activities at an interest level appropriate to teenage pupils. There are no simple answers. Successful schools are casting their nets widely amongst the profile components and Key Stages of all the National Curriculum subjects and making creative and original use of a varied catch of ideas.

All of this has implications for school planning structures. As the subjects of the National Curriculum arrive on teachers' desks, there is a huge task to undertake in rationalising the breadth of curriculum content in schools for pupils with severe learning difficulties. It may not be adequate in the end to give individual teachers subject responsibilities throughout school. The task of monitoring history provision in an all age school, Key Stages 1 to 4, looks thoroughly daunting, for instance. Developing structures for topic management has suggested to some schools that team responsibility for monitoring whole curriculum breadth and balance across age-defined sub-sections of the whole school is more effective. Certainly the team planning involved in integrated schemes of work has produced, for many schools, a useful library of shared teaching records, as well as an enhanced sense of co-operative endeavour.

Ultimately schools will need to develop long term topic plans which sketch out intended coverage over two, three or five years. These long term plans will need to take account of:

- coverage of the relevant content of National Curriculum programmes of study over time;
- a variety of teaching and learning styles;
- elements of the programmes of study which need to be repeated, revisited and reinterpreted as pupils grow older;
- aspects of the programmes of study which link, overlap and inter-relate allowing content-free topics to be scheduled around conceptual themes like 'handling data' (maths, science, English, I.T.); 'sequencing' (history, geography, maths, English); or 'sorting, grouping and classifying' (science, maths, English);
- aspects of the programmes of study which suggest one-off, subject-specific investigations which do not relate easily to other areas of learning (magnetism in science perhaps);

- a variety of topic formats ranging from whole school, whole term; through Key Stage specific, Wednesday afternoons for a month in the lower school; to total immersion all day every day for a week.

Such long term plans should not be seen as straitjackets. The idea of content-free themes would allow teachers to interpret the teaching of essential skills and concepts in an infinite variety of ways. Long term plans may also allow space for discretionary topics on a regular basis, allowing teachers to revise ideas which were hurried over the first time around or to engage in some totally fresh work. Long term topic plans and associated schemes of work would, at least, provide confidence-boosting evidence of the curriculum experienced by pupils throughout a school career.

All of this development is taking place through a time when political pressure from outside schools, LEAs, or other educational establishments is attempting to push school staff firmly in the direction of subject-specific teaching structures and their associated teaching methods. Special schools need not feel that they are alone in seeking creative, imaginative ways of managing the whole curriculum however. Mainstream primary schools continue to engage with the concept of topic planning, although they are seeking more rigorous, curriculum-driven ways of planning and recording their work. In some areas, mainstream schools and LEAs are supporting the creation and delivery of modules of integrated study across Key Stage 2 with great success. In a few areas, there are currently bold attempts being made to devise integrated, cross-curricular courses of work for students in the secondary phase of their mainstream education. In some cases, pioneering work in special schools has informed and stimulated mainstream developments.

An outmoded vision of topic work as an unplanned, ill-executed, unrecorded set of unchallenging and only vaguely educational experiences may be informing the current campaign to re-establish rigidly subject-specific and content-defined teaching. Those of us who believe that the best kinds of learning experiences cannot be so tritely compartmentalised, packaged and imposed now have a real task on our hands. It is our job to take hold of the whole curriculum and to insist that it should be delivered, in all its inter-related complexity, in a variety of stimulating and meaningful ways across the levels and Key Stages. This demonstration of the range of possibilities must encompass planning and record keeping techniques and must acknowledge the full sophistication of the learning process. If we are to reject a simplistic, mechanistic view of education, we need to be in a position to present some powerful alternatives which will stand up to close scrutiny.

**Note:** The author wishes to acknowledge the contributions of the National Curriculum Development Team (SLD), David Banes, Caroline Coles, Lorraine Cooper, Anne Fergusson, Sandra Galloway, Hazel Lawson, Richard Rose, Judy Sebba and Jan Tyne, to the development of the ideas described in this chapter.

160

## References

Ashdown, R., Carpenter, B. and Bovair, K. (1991) *The Curriculum Challenge*. London: Falmer.

Department of Education and Science (1978) *Primary Education in England*. London: HMSO.

Eggleston, J. (1980) 'The drawback of projects.' *The Times Educational Supplement*, 12.9.80.

Eisner, E. (1969) 'Instructional and Expressive Objectives', in W. J. Popham, E. Eisner, H. J. Sullivan and L. L. Tyler, *Instructional Objectives*. American Educational Research Association Monograph Series on Curriculum Evaluation No. 3. Chicago: Rand McNally.

Kent, G. (1968) *Projects in the Primary School*. London: Batsford.

Key, T. (1987) 'A pound for every spaceship: Topic work-planning for a miracle'. *The Times Educational Supplement*, 6.3.87.

Rose, R. (1991) 'A jigsaw approach to group work'. *British Journal of Special Education*, 18, 2, 54–58.

Smith, B. (1991) (Ed.) *Interactive Approaches to Teaching the Core Subjects (the National Curriculum for Pupils with Severe Learning Difficulties)*. Bristol: Lame Duck Publishers.

Thomas, N. (1982) 'Topics in Turmoil', *The Times Educational Supplement*, 1.10.82.

Yendoll, T. (1988) 'Project Work – its Roots and Ancestry', in C. Conner (Ed.) *Topic and Thematic Work in the Primary and Middle Years*. Cambridge: Cambridge Institute of Education.

# CHAPTER 14

# Assessment

*Klaus Wedell*

It is generally recognized that the assessment provisions of the National Curriculum (NC) have been a source of great concern generally, quite apart from their particular impact on pupils with special educational needs (SENs). The assessment procedures specified for the National Curriculum have come to be seen as separated from day to day teaching. During the passage of the Bill which became the 1988 'Education Reform' Act, many warnings were given that the proposals might lead to such a retrograde consequence. The dangers of this separation have long been recognized in special needs education. The booklets on assessment published by the Schools Examination and Assessment Council (SEAC) (SEAC, 1989) do attempt to link assessment with teaching, but are not consistent in this message. Assessment, in the provisions of the 1988 Act, seems to have grown into a monolithic operation. As a result, it is easy to forget that assessment is no more than a means of obtaining answers to questions, and is justified solely by the meaningfulness of the questions asked.

What the Act and many of the subsequent Circulars and other publications do not make clear, is that assessment has to be matched to the variety of different questions which need to be answered. The Circulars themselves already provide some indications that three main groups of questions have to be distinguished:

(1)  teachers' questions about planning the next step for pupils' learning;
(2)  teachers' and parents' questions about their pupils' levels of achievement;
(3)  teachers', parents', governors', LEA administrators', and governments' questions about the quality of education offered.

The 1988 Act proposes two means of assessment to answer all these questions – teacher assessment and assessment by Standard Assessment Tasks (SATs), at four Key Stages (KSs) during a pupil's schooling – when pupils are seven, eleven, fourteen and sixteen. SATs are set by the SEAC, but administered and interpreted by teachers. As is well known, the nature and administration of SATs has undergone radical changes since their initial conception. Before, during and after their piloting in the Summer of 1990, the full implications of the staff time and effort involved in their administration became as apparent to their instigators as it had been all along to educators. As a consequence, the scale of assessment involving SATs has been drastically reduced, and it is likely that the nature of SATs has been modified.

The provisions of the 1988 Act are continuing to be changed, and in such a state of flux it is important that those directly concerned in the education of children guide their decisions and actions in the light of sound educational principles and practice. Special needs education has, over the last fifteen to twenty years, undergone systematic development in the understanding of children's SENs and of ways to meet these. These advances have, to a large extent, been established in statutory documents, including the 1981 Act. As Whetton *et al.* (1991) found in their study of the administration of KS 1 SATs in 1991, those concerned in the education of pupils with SENs have a sound basis for decisions about practice. They will therefore need to consider the 1988 Act's assessment provisions in general, in relation to the three assessment questions mentioned above.

**Planning the next step for pupils' learning**

In general education, and particularly in special needs education, teachers have come to see the curriculum, in its *broad sense*, as the framework for assessing pupils' progress. This curriculum-based assessment has become the means for teachers to obtain information for deciding on the next step for teaching. Assessment goes on as an integral part of teaching. This continuing process clearly cannot be served by SATs assessment, since it occurs only at the four Key Stages in a pupil's schooling. Teacher assessment as proposed could, however, be seen as compatible.

The 1988 Act only provides for teacher assessment within the subjects of the NC. Much has been written about the limitations of the subject-based model of the NC both before and after it was enshrined in the 1988 Act. The conception of the NC has altered considerably, and continues to be changed. The fact that the aims of education, as set out in the 1988 Act, could not be realized within the limits of the NC, has been recognized by the National Curriculum Council (NCC) (NCC, 1990). The point is also acknowledged in the government's booklet 'From Policy to Practice' (DES, 1989). Although schools have been encouraged to adopt Records of Achievement which incorporate a broader view of the curriculum

(Broadfoot *et al.* 1988), this is not a statutory requirement. In its statutory context, assessment by SATs and teacher assessment is still limited to the subject model of the NC.

Within its limits, the NC could, however, make a contribution to curriculum-based assessment. The Attainment Targets (ATs) and their ten levels defined by Statements of Attainments (SoAs) can represent the two dimensions of a curriculum map, on which a pupil's achievement could be located in relation to content and progression. The NC terminology provides a common language in terms of which teachers in ordinary and special schools can communicate about the NC, and teachers within a school are able to discuss whole-school curriculum policies. In the past, many special schools, and some ordinary schools, have built up such curriculum maps for themselves. One of the main findings from one of our recent research projects, was that the capacity of ordinary and special schools to be responsive to pupils' SENs depended on their having effective whole-school curricular policies (Evans *et al.* 1990). Teachers will need to use this stimulus for discussion about the curriculum, to evaluate the NC in terms of what the 'balanced and broadly-based' curriculum promoted by the 1988 Act should entail. It has, of course, still to be established how specifically the curriculum map should be formulated, and this specificity will vary within the range of content over which teachers carry out curriculum-based assessment.

Although the NC provides a two-dimensional view of content and progression, it is important to remember that the NC is itself in a state of development. Unfortunately this point is not made at all clear in the statutory and other publications about the implementation of the 1988 Act. All the Working Parties which produced the proposals for the NC subjects have stressed that these have to be seen as a first best approximation. As everyone knows, there is as yet uncertainty about every aspect of the structure of the NC – the divisions between subjects, the number and scope of ATs within subjects, the appropriateness of dividing ATs into ten levels, and not least, the accuracy with which SoAs define the ten levels, and even whether they are appropriate at all. There has been little or no recognition that these uncertainties await the evaluation of the NC as it comes to be put into practice.

Schools will need to carry out much school-based development of the framework of content and progression suggested by the NC structure, before they can use it as a basis for curriculum-based teacher assessment. It is also important to recognize that this development has to be based on the ATs and not the Programmes of Study (PoSs). While the latter contain ideas for the range of experiences pupils should be offered, and are also compatible with good teaching methods such as project work, teacher assessment relates to the curricular framework underlying these activities, as the recent discussion document on primary education (DES, 1992) also recognized.

164

However, the distinction between the ATs and the PoSs with respect to assessment is also not made sufficiently clearly in the SEAC teacher assessment guides (SEAC, 1989).

## Assessing pupils' levels of achievement

Of all the uncertainties surrounding the structure of the NC, that concerning SoAs probably has the most immediate impact on teacher assessment. Teachers are required to state pupils' achievement levels in relation to SoAs, and yet there is no evidence so far that SoAs:

- actually represent the most relevant sequence in which subject content is learned;
- mark levels which represent equal steps in the sequence of learning;
- mark levels corresponding to achievement at given ages.

If this is the case for all pupils, it certainly becomes a major problem in teacher assessment of those pupils with SENs, who are known to have individual patterns of learning.

The SoAs are, of course, not very tightly defined, and so teachers are likely to interpret them in varying ways. Achieving a consensus about this will be one of the main tasks in a school's development of a whole-school curriculum policy, and is also fundamental to the proposed moderation of teacher assessment procedures. Those producing the SATs have already been faced with the problem of clarifying the definition of the SoAs, and it has not been an easy task.

Pearson (1990) reports that the piloting of the SATs showed that teachers tended to rate pupils' achievement higher on SATs than on teacher assessment, and Whetton et al. (1991) obtained similar findings. These findings do not, of course, indicate which form of assessment was more accurate, since they were not matched against other independent criteria. One possibility is that teachers – especially of pupils with special educational needs, were concerned to make sure that they assessed a pupil fairly in the structured approach required by the SATs, and so persevered more in eliciting a pupil's response than they would have done within teacher assessment. Another possibility is that the SAT procedure had in fact stimulated the teachers to observe a pupil's response more closely, and had led them to a new appreciation of what the pupil was achieving. The School Assessment Folder (SEAC, 1992) warns teachers against modifying SATs in ways which actually make the task easier for the pupil, and Whetton et al. (1991) report that teachers were uncertain about this aspect of assessment.

In the light of these points, it is clear that at present, any statement of achievement in terms of the SoAs must be treated with great caution. SoA levels may not correspond across different ATs, let alone across different subjects. Unfortunately, the Circular on assessment procedures (DES, 1990), and the more recent School Assessment Folder (SEAC, 1992) does not warn about this. Both documents give guidance on aggregating pupils' levels of achievement in ATs at KSs as though SoAs were proven units of measurement.

In principle, stating a pupil's achievement within the progression of the different content areas of the curriculum is undoubtedly most meaningful, and provides a particularly suitable way to describe the achievement of pupils with SENs. A considerable degree of development will need to have occurred before the NC structure can be reliably used in this way.

### Assessing the quality of the education offered

One of the main purposes of the introduction of SATs, was that they would introduce some uniformity of assessment across schools, and so realise the 1988 Act's expressed aim, in the words of the then Secretary of State for Education, of introducing competition between schools on the basis of pupils' aggregate achievement within the NC. Quite apart from the uncertainties of these aggregates as mentioned above, assessing the quality of a school's education will, of course, need to take account of much more than pupils' achievement within the subjects of the NC. This is not the place to consider the general educational appropriateness of these policies, but it is necessary to examine their relevance for the assessment of pupils with SENs.

It is obvious that a school's effectiveness is indicated more directly by the progress pupils make over a period of time – the 'value added' by a school. It is also open to question whether average figures, whether of attainment or of progress, are the best way to evaluate a school. Furthermore, information on the achievement levels of a representative sample of pupils could provide an adequate and decidedly more cost effective indication than testing all the pupils.

The limited value of NC assessment for evaluating teaching in schools has also been mentioned in the NFER investigation of reading standards (NFER, 1991). The researchers comment that NC data will provide some data over time, but only in a global form. For an appropriately detailed picture, a system of specific monitoring is required, such as was used by the previous Assessment of Performance Unit.

All of these points are particularly relevant when it comes to evaluating schools' effectiveness in providing for pupils with SENs. There seems little disagreement that the effectiveness of schools in this regard should be assessed, but there is considerable doubt about how it should best be done. It is also clear that for all pupils, and particularly for those with SENs, achievement on performance in the NC alone would be an inadequate indicator.

Most importantly, however, it has to be recognized that the purpose of evaluating schools is not to encourage competition, but rather to identify those schools which are not adequately meeting pupils' SENs, so that measures can be taken to rectify this. Unfortunately, the policy of promoting competition seems to be paramount, and its effect on distorting the proper evaluation of schools' effectiveness in meeting pupils' SENs is reflected in a passage in the government's booklet *From policy to practice* (DES, 1989). The booklet asserts that schools may fear that 'the overall picture of the attainment for their pupils will suffer because the attainments of some pupils with SENs are included'. The booklet therefore suggests that 'information about the attainment of some pupils with SENs might be excluded from the aggregate figures which must be published'. The implications of such a suggestion raise two basic doubts – whether there is in fact an intention that schools should be evaluated for the education they offer to *each one* of their pupils, and whether there is a commitment to realizing the NC as a curriculum for all. Its implications could certainly lead to a direct contravention of governors' responsibilities under section 2 (5) of the 1981 Act.

So far, I have been concerned with examining the general indications of the 1988 Act's provisions for assessing pupils with SENs. It is now time to look at the implications for pupils according to the nature of their SENs.

**The impact of SENs on assessment**

The problems of making the NC itself accessible to pupils with SENs have been well rehearsed, and they apply in a similar fashion to assessment. There is, of course, much more scope for making teacher assessment accessible to pupils than assessment by SATs. SEAC has, from the start, expressed concern that maximum accessibility to the SATS procedures should be ensured for pupils with SENs, but Pearson (1990) reported that very little work had been done on developing the necessary modifications. The reference notes provided by SEAC for the 1992 KS 1 assessment include suggestions to teachers about ways of administering SATs to pupils with visual, motor and communication problems. However, they do not go into the fact that 'translating' the assessment measures to bypass mediational barriers may well radically change both the nature of a task and its level of difficulty. This has been investigated, for example, by Halden (1990) in relation to hearing impaired pupils using BSL.

The reference notes also mention adaptations for pupils who 'for one reason or another, need extra support in the classroom' and who 'need extra thought, planning or attention in order to have a fair chance to show what they can do in the SAT'. This is taken to refer to pupils whose attainment is below or around level 1, who have concentration, behaviour or social problems, or who lack confidence.

Bangs (1990) raised important points about the assessment of pupils with emotional and behaviour problems. Quoting from an NUT survey of teachers who took part in the trials of SATs, he reports that teachers found that the practicalities of administering SATs in the classroom meant that they were less able to respond to individual pupils' needs. Those with behaviour problems were thus inevitably less well supported during their work, with potentially detrimental effects on their performance.

Assessing pupils with learning difficulties, particularly severe and complex ones, presents major problems. The most obvious question arises about the assessment of pupils of compulsory school age whose achievement within the NC content is below level one. It is proposed that these pupils should be regarded as 'working towards' level one. Fagg *et al.* (1990) have developed what they term 'milestones' in a downward extension of some of the NC ATs in the core subjects. These offer markers for assessing pupils' progress and avoid the need for a assessments formulated repeatedly as 'working towards level one' at successive key stages. However, these downward extensions involve the authors in complex attempts to interpret the ATs in a way which is compatible with their definition in the NC. As Ware (1990) points out, it is difficult to know when such attempts become so tenuous that they distort curricular intentions. There is clearly a paradox here, since the NC is, in the words of the title of the NCC publication on special needs, meant to be a 'curriculum for all' (NCC, 1989).

For pupils working within the NC levels, the intention of SEAC apparently is that at each KS, SATs should make it possible to state levels of achievement from one upwards. Even if this is achieved, one is led to wonder what might be the meaningfulness of the NC offered to pupils with more severe learning difficulties. This raises issues about the informal and statutory modification and disapplication of the NC, which I have discussed elsewhere (Wedell, 1990a) and which are beyond the scope of this paper. It is important to mention however, that there is apparently no intention that pupils should be disapplied from assessment at any KS, unless they have been exempted from the corresponding NC content. There had been some concern that ordinary schools might feel themselves pressured by the competitive influences of the 1988 Act mentioned above, to invoke the Section 19 temporary disapplication provisions for pupils who would be likely to achieve poorly at a KS.

Both Pearson (1990) and Fagg *et al.* (1990) seem to agree with my suggestion (Wedell, 1990b) that in the foreseeable future, the main way to achieve the widest access to NC assessment will be to abandon SAT assessment where it is felt that this will not provide an accurate and relevant measure of a pupil's achievement, and to use teacher assessment alone. This seems entirely compatible with article 6 (2) (b) of the KS 1 Orders (DES, 1990). However, the explanation of this article in Circular 9/90 (paragraph

23) seems to put additional constraints on this course of action. The paragraph implies that SAT assessment can only be discounted once it has been carried out, and when the teacher and the head teacher then both judge that it 'is not a true reflection of the pupil's attainments'. The SEAC, in the School Assessment Folder for KS 1 SAT assessment for 1992 (SEAC, 1992), appear to follow the lines of Circular 9/90. It also appears to be permissible for the pupil to be exempted from assessment through the Section 18 or 19 procedures, in the light of difficulties encountered in applying the SAT procedure, and for a retrospective decision to be made that 'the attainment target itself is not a suitable focus for learning in the child's curriculum'. The writers of the Folder regard this eventuality as exceptional, and well they might. It seems extraordinary that anyone should suppose that teachers would not notice that a part of a curriculum was inappropriate for a pupil, until they were faced with a Key Stage SAT.

## Conclusion

As Pearson (1990) has stated, the work of applying the procedures for NC assessment to pupils with SENs has hardly begun. This is not surprising, since the problem has existed within education in general for a long time. From one point of view, we should probably welcome the fact that the aspiration to give all pupils an entitlement to the NC has now raised the issue in a more urgent form.

Much concern about the 1988 Act's assessment provisions for pupils with SENs appears to result from the educational inadequacies of the procedures in general. The impact of SAT assessment has, of course, been somewhat lessened, following the reduction in the range of the NC to which the SATs are to be applied. However, the retreat from the objective of making the SAT procedure compatible with day to day teaching has made the remaining procedures less educationally relevant.

It will be interesting to see how policy on SATs develops. There appears to be a growing realization that the universal administration of SATs in their present form meets neither the requirements of individual assessment, nor of the monitoring of standards. One would hope that it will become increasingly obvious that a financial investment in appropriate moderation of teacher assessment within and between school staffs offers considerably greater scope both for a development of curriculum-based assessment, and for curriculum development generally. This would help teachers to monitor pupils' progress more closely, and so make a major contribution to the recognition of pupils' SENs, and to evaluating attempts to help them.

## References

Bangs, J. (1990) 'Assess through teachers, not tests'. *British Journal of Special Education*, **17**, 4, 133-135.

Broadfoot, P. *et al.* (1988) *Records of achievement – the report of the national evaluation of pilot schemes.* London: HMSO.

Department of Education and Science (1989) *From policy to practice.* London: DES.

Department of Education and Science (1990) *The education (National Curriculum) assessment arrangements for English, Mathematics and Science order 1990.* London: DES.

Department of Education and Science (1992) *Primary Practice – a discussion paper.* London: DES.

Evans, P., Ireson, J., Redmond, P. and Wedell, K. (1990) *Pathways to Progress.* Institute of Education, University of London.

Fagg, S., Aherne, P., Skelton, S. and Thornber, A. (1990) *Entitlement for all in practice.* London: David Fulton.

Halden, J. (1990) *The National Curriculum: towards a British Sign Language attainment target.* Unpublished Master's Thesis, Institute of Education, University of London.

National Curriculum Council (1989) *A curriculum for all.* York: NCC.

National Curriculum Council (1990) *The whole curriculum.* York: NCC.

Pearson, L, (1990) 'What have the pilot SATs taught us?' *British Journal of Special Education,* 17, 4, 130–132.

Schools Examination and Assessment Council (1990) SEAC specification for SATs approved, *SEAC Recorder,* 6, 1–2.

Schools Examination and Assessment Council (1991) *Key Stage 1 National Curriculum Assessment: core subject standard assessment tasks for 1992: reference notes.* Schools Examination and Assessment Council.

Schools Examination and Assessment Council (1992) Key Stage 1 assessment folder. Schools Examination and Assessment Council.

Ware, J. (1990) 'The National Curriculum for pupils with severe learning difficulties', in: Daniels, H. and Ware, J. (eds) *Special educational needs and the National Curriculum.* London: Kogan Page.

Wedell, K. (1990a) 'The 1988 Act and current principles of special educational needs, in: Daniels, H. and Ware, J. (eds) *Special educational needs and the National Curriculum.* London: Kogan Page.

Wedell, K. (1990b) 'Question marks', *Times Educational Supplement,* (28.9.90).

Whetton, C. *et al.* (1991) *An evaluation of the 1991 National Curriculum Assessment: Report 3, Further evidence on the SAT.* NFER/BGC Consortium.

# CONCLUSION

# The National Curriculum in the Context of Change

*Keith Bovair and Graham Upton*

Breadth, balance, relevance and differentiation are four words which encapsulate the challenge for educators who desire to ensure a curriculum for all. As evidenced in the previous chapters, professionals in the field of special education have been active in this drive for entitlement. However, the movement towards such goals is relatively recent. 'Pre-Warnock', special education was characterized by care, concern and segregation and it has only been since the late 1970's that there have been major calls for integration. Even then, curriculum development has been decribed by Swann (1988) as being dominated by deficit theories; and assuming that if a child can't do something in one setting, then he/she can't do it at all, and criticized by Bovair (1989) as being inappropriately weighted towards language and number.

Changes in the understanding of the curricular needs of pupils with special educational needs have been occurring since the early 1980's. Influential in stimulating the process of change have been various. HMI reports such as *Curriculum from to 5 to 16* (1985) which argued that:

> A school's curriculum consists of all those activities designed or encouraged within its organisational framework to promote the intellectual, personal, social and physical development of its pupils. It includes not only the formal programme of lessons, but also the informal programme of so-called extracurricular activities as well as those features which produce the school's ethos, such as the quality of relationships, the concern for equality of opportunity, the values exemplified in the way that the school sets about its task and the way in which it is organised and managed (Whitaker, 1988, p. 20).

The significance of this statement in relation to special educational needs was stated by Whitaker as being that

...such a definition promotes an inclusive view of curriculum design and suggests an altogether more holistic approach than we have been traditionally used to. It was a statement that helped encourage the opportunity for inclusion of pupils with special educational needs into the mainstream of curriculum opportunity by pointing to 'the equality of opportunity' (p. 21).

Also influential in encouraging a broader view of the curriculum was the involvement of special schools in national initiatives which forced them to re-examine their practice and drew them out of their often self-imposed isolation. The most important initiative in this regard was the Technical, Vocational and Educational Initiative (TVEI) which:

> encouraged skills of direct value at work, equipping students to enter the world of employment, to develop problem solving skills and establishing a bridge from school to work through relevant activities. It also created a forum in which special schools sat alongside secondary schools and further education to work collaboratively on projects within the guide-lines of TVEI. Money was made available to establish in-service training (TVEI Related In-service Training – TRIST) for all staff involved, and it was here that a strong common ground was well established, leading to exchanges of ideas, of resources and of students and staff between the different kinds of establishments. Other ventures into curriculum development followed in the wake of this initiative. Collaboration over GCSE course work and shared facilities were assisted by a new way of grouping schools. *Clusters* of schools were set up to work together in their education communities and when primary schools entered into this world under the guise of Grant Related In-service Training (GRIST), (often considered by educators as TRIST without money) a healthy relationship benefited all children (Bovair, 1992).

## The introduction of the National Curriculum

The impact of the National Curriculum, however, had a dramatic impact on this process. Initial reactions to the proposal contained in the 1988 Education Reform Act were ones of fear that the interests of children with special educational need would not be well served by its introduction (see, for example Upton, 1990). The original Bill had only one reference to special educational needs and one to special schools and the Bill was seen by many as being likely to destroy the changes which had occurred in the understanding and treatment of children with special educational needs since the 1944 Education Act and which had been reinforced by the Warnock Report and the 1981 Education Act.

The principal argument advanced for the introduction of the National Curriculum was the expectation that it would lead to an improvement in academic standards and we were assured that the National Curriculum was for every pupil and that it was flexible enough to permit wide participation by pupils with special needs without compromising its breadth and balance (NCC, 1989b). Many, however, were not convinced that this was possible. For some, the introduction of a national curriculum with its specific requirements for subject study was seen as a threat to the flexibility with which special schools and classes had been able to work. Equally, many were concerned about the relevance of traditional subjects to children who present severe learning or behavioural difficulties and the effects which the introduction of an apparently narrowly conceived academic curriculum would have on the teaching of cross curricular issues such as social and life skills.

In the event, many of these concerns were allayed and as time has gone on concern has focused more on the prospect of the National Curriculum not being applied to children with special educational needs than on its relevance. Recently the focus of attention of most special educators has moved to matters concerning the implementation of the curriculum rather than issues of principle. For most schools and most teachers the curriculum is now reality and energy has focused on its development and adaptation. This is reflected in the HMI report, *National Curriculum and Special Needs* (DES, 1991) where, among other things, it is stated that its survey of ordinary and special schools revealed that:

- there was widespread commitment by teachers to planning for maximum possible access to the National Curriculum for all children;
- most schools...were reviewing the breadth and balance of the curriculum for pupils with SEN...(and)...addressing gaps and limitations revealed by such reviews;
- curriculum review in preparation for implementing the National Curriculum had already led to some pupils with SEN being given a broader and better balanced curriculum than previously.

Unfortunately the curriculum guide-lines which have been produced by the various working groups have not always provided concrete guidance for curriculum adaptation or development needed to meet special educational needs. Some help with this was provided by the National Curriculum Council in *A Curriculum for All* (NCC, 1989a). This begins by repeating some of the principles of participation outlined in earlier publications but goes on to discuss what the council regards as essential in making the National Curriculum accessible to pupils with special educational needs. For teachers concerned with the practicalities of implementation it also provided case study material to illustrate ways in which pupils with special needs can participate in science, maths and primary English programmes of study. More recently, accounts of good practice, written by practitioners have begun to appear (see, for example, Ackerman and Mount, 1991; Aherne *et al*. 1990a; 1990b; Fagg *et al*. 1990a; 1990b) and it is in this context that the contributions to the present volume are particularly valuable. They have elaborated clearly how the criteria of breadth, balance, relevance and differentiation can be met across the full range of the National Curriculum, and that the National Curriculum is flexible enough to permit wide participation by pupils with special needs.

## The National Curriculum in context

Notwithstanding the progress which has been made, the realisation of the aim to provide access to a broad, balanced, relevant and differentiated curriculum is not solely dependent on the ability of a teacher or a group of teachers to adapt or develop a curriculum that meets the needs of specific children. It depends heavily on the context in which that teacher or group of teachers works. The importance of this was recognised in *A Curriculum for All* (NCC, 1989a) where in addition to the advice which it provides on curriculum development and adaptation are contained valuable comments about issues of school policy and organisation. In particular, it argued that:

(a) it was essential for schools to have clearly defined school policies on special educational needs on the grounds that, in both ordinary and special schools, good practice is most likely to be advanced when all members of staff are committed to the same aims: providing a broad, balanced, relevant and differentiated curriculum, and raising standards for each of the pupils they teach;

(b) in order to ensure that special educational needs are adequately met in ordinary schools it is necessary for:
    - all staff to know which pupils have special educational needs, the nature of their needs and how best to meet their needs;
    - adequate resources, support and training to be available to staff;
    - a designated member of staff to be responsible for co-ordinating school policy in relation to special educational needs;
    - the effects of the National Curriculum on pupils with special educational needs to be monitored and evaluated.

(c) pupils with special educational needs are likely to have even stronger needs than other pupils for:
    - positive attitudes from school staff who are determined to ensure their fullest participation in the National Curriculum;
    - partnerships with teachers which encourage them to become active learners, helping them to plan, build and evaluate their own learning programmes wherever possible;
    - a climate of warmth and support in which self-confidence and self-esteem can grow and in which pupils feel valued and able to risk making mistakes as they learn, without fear of criticism;
    - emphasis on profiles of achievement which encourage self-assessment and which record all that pupils have achieved and experienced in both the National Curriculum and the curriculum as a whole;

 - home-school partnerships which enable families to support the teaching programmes for the child with special educational needs.

The value of a whole-school approach and issues which influence the effective operation of such a system have been further elaborated in publications such as those of Ainscow and Florek (1989) and Ramasut (1989). These all support the importance for those involved in managing curriculum development of an awareness of the broad contextual issues which impinge on curriculum content and teaching and learning. Such suggestions as those cited above from *A Curriculum for All* may provide potentially invaluable ammunition for anyone working to establish good practice and more positive school policies towards children with special educational needs.

## Looking towards the future

The compilation of papers in this book highlight currently topical areas of interest in the National Curriculum. The contributors have all attempted to identify issues which are central to good curricula practice in this climate of rapid educational change. A key question must be, how these concerns will alter and what new issues will emerge over the next ten years which might effect the ability of teachers and schools to give all children access to the National Curriculum. What will be the key curricula challenges as we move towards the twenty first century?

## Local management of schools

One issue which is with us already and the resolution to which may have far reaching effects on curriculum access is the local management of schools and the changing role of Local Authorities and the support services which they currently provide. The introduction of local school management in the 1988 Education Reform Act means that each maintained school will in due course become a separate budget centre. While this has been widely welcomed by schools for the freedom it gives them to respond quickly and effectively to rapidly changing circumstances there are fears that it may affect the quality of provision available to children with special educational needs, particularly those located in ordinary schools. Under local management schemes LEAs will have discretion whether or not to delegate provision for pupils subject to statements under the 1988 Act who are in ordinary schools. Where provision is delegated this will be reflected in the school's budget and schools will have freedom to consider how best to deploy those resources. The LEA, however, will remain responsible for identifying, assessing and determining the provision required for individual pupils and for the conduct of annual reviews and mandatory reassessments. So far so good.

The arrangements which apply to children regarded as having special educational needs but who are not statemented are less satisfactory. DES circular 22/89 notes the 'need for L.E.A.s and governors to take steps to satisfy parents of children without statements that appropriate educational provision will be available in schools to meet their particular needs' (DES, 1989, para 16, p. 7); but no firmer guidance than this has been provided on how this appropriate provision might be financed or monitored.

A fear lurking in the minds of some is the possibility that Governors may not be as sympathetic towards children with special educational needs as Local Authorities, with their broader political bases, have had to be. This is not to suggest that the Governors of any school are likely to set out deliberately to take decisions which are prejudicial to the interest of children with special needs. However, under local school management, school budgets will be pupil-driven with school finances dependent on enrolment. When this is taken in conjunction with the fact that parental choice of schools, in future, is likely to be influenced by a more specific knowledge of attainment levels than has been the case in the past, there are grounds for concern. Thus, if parents see schools in which the level of attainments reached in the National Curriculum are high *as better schools*, as would seem likely, then enrolment in those schools might grow at the expense of others; equally, the intake characteristics of pupils could change over time with the result that some schools might emerge as quasi-grammar schools while others acquire a less favourable status.

In other words, schools' reputations may be won or lost on the basis of their pupils' attainments. While the attainments of pupils who are the subjects of statements may be excluded from a schools' profile of results, this does not apply to the larger group of children with special educational needs who are not statemented. As Willey (1990) has pointed out there is a real danger that the ERA will encourage the idea that pupils with special educational needs are a disadvantage to a schools' academic results and, very importantly, to its use of teaching resources (p. 136). Whether these fears are realistic, or whether they are groundless, must await the test of time but the cause for concern is real enough.

Such fears become even more pressing when seen in the context of other pressures on school budgets. It is not clear at this stage, for example, whether or not the funds allocated to schools will be adequate to allow them to meet the additional costs which will now accrue to schools instead of LEAs (e.g. day to day budgetary control and management) and the additional costs which the operation of the National Curriculum will impose on schools (e.g. additional record keeping, testing and assessment, setting up new recording schemes). If it is not, then this will amount to a diminution of existing funding and the question which will then arise is where will schools make the savings this will require. **Willey (1990), a primary school headteacher, has noted that:**

> For two terms now, because of administrative work imposed by the E.R.A., I have been unable to spend the customary two to three sessions a week working with class teachers to give extra help to pupils whose minor learning difficulties are more likely to become major ones if extra support is withdrawn. (p. 137)

Links between special and ordinary schools which have been advocated as a means by which special schools may extend their curriculum provision by using the resources of ordinary schools, may equally be threatened. Not unreasonably, ordinary schools might be reluctant to become involved in such schemes unless some means can be found to recompense them for the use of their resources by children for whom they are not funded.

Another issue of particular importance is the effect which LMS may have on support services. Again, the problem is not so much with those children who are the subject of a statement under the 1981 Act but more with the larger group of children with special needs who are not subjects of statements. Thus far it is not clear to what extent LEAs will maintain provision centrally or to what extent LMS will create an open market situation dominated by the ability and willingness of schools to pay for such services. At risk is the support provided by Advisory Teachers and the School Psychological Services within Education but equally so is the support provided by agencies such as Health and Social Services. The final solution may be a mixed economy in which private practice may compete for school business with Government agencies but to what extent schools will be able to afford such services at what will presumably have to be charged at full costs is not yet known. Once again children with special educational needs may turn out to be less well served than they are now.

## Beyond a National Curriculum

The need for rapid and continuous curriculum change will be highlighted by the continued development of relationships within Europe. Having had little time to adjust to the concept of a National Curriculum the suggestion that this may be superseded by European initiatives will not be welcomed by some teachers. However, this would seem inevitably to be the case as international borders are relaxed with the emergence of a United Europe. Joint ventures in meeting the educational needs of children who have special educational needs will be needed to allow for the development of curricula which Thousand and Villa (1991) and Wiggins (1989) have suggested will increasingly have to address interdependent and international societal trends. This will provide the opportunity to further extend the boundaries of the curriculum and foster the emergence of an international curriculum which will become more and more accessible as technology is further enhanced.

Equally obviously, the curriculum offered in all schools and in all phases of education will have to change to keep pace with the exponential growth of information and new technological studies. Alley (1985) cited by Thousand and Villa (1991) highlights the short 'half-life' of knowledge because of which he argues that it is vital that we are all open to the possibility of continual and continuous change in the curriculum. If we are to cope with the pace of change and respond positively to it Wiggins (1989) argues that there will be a need and ability to

- Suspend disbelief;
- Listen;
- Question;
- Be open to new and strange ideas;
- Support a community ethic (peer advocate/buddy/tutor);
- Develop skills to communicate with a diverse population from the global community;
- Learn how to learn;
- Re-examine regularly the 'core' curriculum.

Many of these qualities can be seen to be in place already in the special needs community but the introduction of each new piece of technology enhances communication around the world and makes it increasingly important that we remain open to new ideas. While this sounds an obvious conclusion it is important to recognise that responding positively to constant change can induce a great deal of stress amongst those who are involved in it. It is important that teachers and schools develop adequate coping mechanisms to ensure that they do feel able to respond positively to new initiatives and are not tempted to retreat behind the traditions of the past. Peer support is one possible means of meeting the pressures of change while clusters' or 'consortia' of schools, working together, collectively and creatively in the areas of the curriculum and staff development may provide a key to the management of further change.

## Conclusion

In many ways the present volume can be seen as a celebration of the triumph of the special educational needs community in responding positively to the introduction of a National Curriculum which initially seemed to have little relevance to its interests. That it has done so is, in turn, a reflection of the quality of the people who are involved in the field. It is clear from what has been written in this book, and elsewhere, that the National Curriculum can be an appropriate vehicle to meet the needs of all children. Whether it will do that remains to be seen. It is too early yet to judge how effectively it will be implemented. Furthermore, in this chapter, an attempt has been made to point out that much depends on contextual influences not directly related to the National Curriculum itself.

It has been suggested also that a climate of continued rapid change is likely to characterise education for some time to come. The extent to which the educational needs of all children are met will depend in large measure on a continued ability to respond to fresh initiatives wherever they originate but perhaps more important will be the extent to which special educators are able to be pro-active as well as reactive. There is a danger that much that has been achieved so far in responding to the National Curriculum may be lost as a reuslt of inadequate support both within and outside schools. There is much good in the field of special educational needs but being good at something does not necessarily mean that it will endure. There is a need, perhaps now more than at any other time, to be aware of the need to speak out for the interests of pupils with special educational needs.

What then are the issues about which action is needed? The HMI survey, *National Curriculum and Special Needs*, which was referred to above highlights five issues in its concluding section which appear particularly pertinent to the present authors. Roughly summarised these suggest the need to press for

- regular curriculum review in both ordinary and special schools to ensure that access to the National Curriculum is safeguarded for all pupils;
- curriculum reviews to include due attention to school organisation as well as direct curriculum concerns;
- continued and enhanced opportunities for in-service training;
- adequate resources and accommodation for implementing the National Curriculum both in ordinary and special schools and with statemented and non-statemented children;
- guidance and support to allow schools to develop expertise in curriculum related assessment and recording of pupils' achievement.

There are probably many other issues which could be added to this list and many more that will emerge with the passage of time but in some ways the specific issues are less important than the recognition that action is needed. And perhaps even more important than the recognition that action is needed is the need to communicate about the issues involved and the action that is needed. As a professional group special educators are not good at sharing their experiences and it is hoped that, if the present books achieves nothing else, it may encourage others to write about their ideas and their experiences. Many examples of good practice unfortunately lie locked away in the minds of those who deliver it. At the present time it is arguably more important than it ever has been for more of that knowledge to be shared.

Finally let us return to the Warnock Report. This provides a framework which can be used as guide to all curriculum development the following summary of which is as fitting a way as any to end the present volume:

> We hold that education has certain long-term goals, that it has a general point or purpose which can be definitely though generally stated. The goals are two-fold. They are first to enlarge a child's knowledge, experience and imaginative

understanding and thus his awareness of moral values and capacity for enjoyment and secondly to enable him to enter the world after formal education is over as an active participant in society and a responsible contributor to it, capable of achieving as much independence as possible. (DES, 1978, para 1.4)

## References

Ackerman, D. and Mount, H. (1991) *Literacy for All*. London: David Fulton.
Aherne, P., Thornber, A., Fagg, S. and Skelton, S. (1990a) *Communication for All*. London: David Fulton.
Aherne, P., Thornber, A., Fagg, S. and Skelton, S. (1990b) *Mathematics for All*. London: David Fulton.
Ainscow, M. and Florek, A. (1949) *Special Educational Needs: Towards a Whole School Approach*. London: David Fulton.
Bovair, K. (1989) 'The Special School, A Part of, not Apart From the Educational System', in D. Baker and K. Bovair (eds) *Making the Special School Ordinary, Vol. One, Models for the Developing Special School*. Lewes: Falmer Press.
Bovair, K. (1992) 'Curriculum and Special Educational Needs', in R. Gulliford and G. Upton (eds) *Special Educational Needs*. London: Routledge.
Department of Education and Science (1978) *Special Educational Needs*. London: HMSO.
Department of Education and Science (1985) *Curriculum for 5 to 16*. London: HMSO.
Department of Education and Science (1989) *Assessments and Statements of Special Educational Needs: Procedures within the Education, Health and Social Services*. Circular 22/89. London: DES.
Department of Education and Science (1991) *National Curriculum and Special Needs*. London: HMSO.
Fagg, S., Aherne, P., Skelton, S. and Thornber, A. (1990a) *Entitlement for All in Practice*. London: David Fulton.
Fagg, S., Skelton, S., Aherne, P. and Thornber, S. (1990b) *Science for All*. London: David Fulton.
Haviland, J., (1988) *Take Care, Mr. Baker*. London: Fourth Estate.
National Curriculum Council (1989a) *Curriculum Guidance 2: A Curriculum for All*. York: National Curriculum Council.
National Curriculum Council (1989b) Circular No. 5, York: National Curriculum Council.
Ramasut, A. (ed) *Whole School Approaches to Special Needs*. Lewes: Falmer Press.
Swann, W. (1988) 'Learning difficulties and curriculum reform: integration or differentiation?' in G. Thomas and A. Feiler (eds) *Planning for Special Needs*. Oxford: Basil Blackwell.
Thousand, J. and Villa, R. (1991) 'A futuristic view of the REI: a response to Jenkins, Pious and Jewell' *Exceptional Children*, **57**, 6, 556–562.
Upton, G. (1990) 'The Education Reform Act and Special Educational Needs' *Newsletter of the Association for Child Psychology and Psychiatry*. **12**, 5, 3–9.
Whitaker, P. 'Curriculum considerations' in D. Hicks (ed) *Education for Peace*. London: Routledge.
Wiggins, G. (1989) 'The futility of trying to teach everything of importance' *Educational Leadership*, **47**, 3, 44–59.
Willey, M. (1990) L.M.S.: 'A Rising Sense of Alarm'. *British Journal of Special Education*, **16**, 4, 136–138.